WRITTEN
ON CLAY AND STONE

Ancient Near Eastern Studies Presented to Krystyna Szarzyńska

WRITTEN ON CLAY AND STONE

Ancient Near Eastern Studies Presented to
Krystyna Szarzyńska
on the Occasion of her 80th Birthday

edited by

Jan Braun
Krystyna Łyczkowska
Maciej Popko
Piotr Steinkeller

AGADE
Warsaw 1998

01-691 Warszawa, Gdańska 22, Poland
e-mail: kapelus@plearn.edu.pl

Graphics and cover design: Agata Nalborczyk

ISBN 83-87111-07-4

PREFACE

On this day Krystyna Szarzyńska celebrates her eightieth birthday. To recognize this happy occasion, her friends and colleagues in Poland and aboard are offering her this collection of articles. In this small way we wish to pay tribute to her numerous contributions to the field of Sumerology and to show our appreciation for the warmth, kindness, and good humor she has been so generous to share with us.

During the more than thirty-five years of her scholarly work, Krystyna has touched on many different Sumerological issues, but, regardless of the specific topic, her ultimate goal has always been to further the understanding of the earliest cuneiform script, one of the most difficult and challenging areas of Assyriological studies. Her life story not that of a typical philologist. For many years she worked as an agronomist in the Polish Ministry of Agriculture. But as that work agreed with neither her passion for the humanities nor her inborn scholarly temperament, she decided, at the age of forty-three, to go back to school, this time enrolling in the Department of Ancient Oriental Philologies at the Warsaw University. Having chosen Sumerian as her specialization, from the onset she devoted herself – heart and soul – to the study of the beginnings of cuneiform. The result of this work has been an uninterrupted flow of publications which have significantly improved our knowledge of the earliest Mesopotamian script.

Always kind, always willing to be of help to others, generous beyond any measure, a perfect friend – she has endeared herself to a host of colleagues and students.

We wish you, dear Krystyna, a very Happy Birthday, hoping that you will continue to enrich us with your work and friendship for many years to come!

–

The editors express their appreciation to all those whose help and cooperation enabled the publication of this volume. First and foremost we extend our thanks to Magdalena Kapełuś for her indispensable editorial work.

Warsaw, May 19th, 1998 The Editors

TABLE OF CONTENTS

List of Abbreviations

AAS	J.-P. Grégoire, *Archives administratives sumériennes*, Paris 1970
AfO	Archiv für Orientforschung
AHw	W. von Soden, *Akkadisches Handwörterbuch*, Wiesbaden 1965ff.
Ai.	lexical series ki.KI.KAL.bi.šè = *ana ittišu*, publ. MSL 1
AION	Annali. Rivista del Dipartimento di Studi Asiatici e del Dipartimento di Studi e Ricerche su Africa e Paesi Arabi. Istituto Universitario Orientale di Napoli
ANET	J. Pritchard et al., *Ancient Near Eastern Texts relating to the Old Testament*, Princeton 1955
AnOr	Analecta Orientalia
AOAT	Alter Orient und Altes Testament
AoF	Altorientalische Forschungen
ARET	Archivi reali di Ebla. Testi
ARM(T)	Archives royales de Mari (Textes)
ARRIM	Annual Review of the Royal Inscriptions of Mesopotamia Project
ASJ	Acta Sumerologica
ATU	A. Falkenstein, *Archaische Texte aus Uruk*, Berlin-Leipzig 1936
BaghMitt	Baghdader Mitteilungen
BBVO	Berliner Beiträge zum Vorderen Orient
BDHP	L. Waterman, *Bussines documents of the Hammurapi period from the British Museum*, London 1916
BE	Babylonian Expedition of the University of Pennsylvania
BIN	Babylonian inscriptions in the collection of J. B. Nies
BiOr	Bibliotheca Orientalis
BM	tablets in the collections of the British Museum
CAD	*The Assyrian Dictionary of the Oriental Institute of the University of Chicago*
CBS	tablets in the collections of the University Museum of the University of Pennsylvania, Philadelphia
CHM	Cahiers d'histoire mondiale
CRAIB	Comptes rendus de l'Académie des Inscriptions et Belles-Lettres
CT	Cuneiform Texts from Babylonian Tablets
CTH	E. Laroche, *Catalogue des Textes Hittites*, Paris 1971
CTN	Cuneiform Texts from Nimrud
Emar	D. Arnaud, *Recherches au pays d'Aštata*, Paris 1985-1987
FAOS	Freiburger altorientalische Studien

GDD	N. Schneider, *Die Geschäftsurkunden aus Drehem und Djoha in den Staatlichen Museen (VAT) zu Berlin in Autographie und mit systematischen Wörterindices herausgegeben*, OrSP 47-49 (1930)
HAV	*Hilprecht anniversary volume, studies in Assyriology and archaeology dedicated to Hermann V. Hilprecht upon the twenty-fifth anniversary of his doctorate and his fiftieth birthday (July 28) by his colleagues, friends and admirers*, Leipzig, 1909
IM	tablets in the collections of the Iraq Museum, Baghdad
JAOS	Journal of the American Oriental Society
JCS	Journal of Cuneiform Studies
JEOL	Jaarbericht van het Vooraziatisch-Egyptisch Genootschap „Ex Oriente Lux"
JFieldA	Journal of Field Archaeology
JNES	Journal of Near Eastern Studies
KBo	Keilschrifttexte aus Boghazköi
KDD	N. Schneider, *Das Drehem- und Djohaarchiv*, 2. Heft: *Der Götterkult* (1. Teil), OrSP 18 (1925)
KUB	Keilschrifturkunden aus Boghazköi
LAK	A. Deimel, *Liste der archaichen Keilschriftziechen* (WVDOG 40), Leipzig 1922
MARI	Mari. Annales de Recherches Interdisciplinaires
MB	Middle Babylonian
MDP	Mémoires de la Délégation en Perse
MEE	Materiali Epigrafici di Ebla
MIO	Mitteilungen des Instituts für Orientforschung
MSL	Materialien zum sumerischen Lexikon
MVN	Materiali per il vocabolario neosumerico
NABU	Nouvelles Assyriologiques Brèves et Utilitaires
NCBT	tablets in the Newell collection of Babylonian tablets
NFT	*Nouvelles fouilles de Tello*, Paris 1910
NSGU	A. Falkenstein, *Die neusumerischen Gerichtsurkunden*, München 1956-1957
OA	Oriens Antiquus
OB	Old Babylonian
OPBF 2	Adele Berlin, *Enmerkar and Ensuḫkešdanna* (Occasional Publications of Babylonian Fund, 2), Philadelphia 1979
OECT	Oxford editions of cuneiform texts
OIP	Oriental Institute Publications
OLA	Orientalia Lovaniensia Analecta
Or	Orientalia
PBS	Publications of the Babylonian Section, University Museum, University of Pennsylvania
PSD	Philadelphia Sumerian Dictionary

PTS	Princeton Theological Seminary
QS	Quaderni di Semitistica
RA	Revue d'assyriologie et d'archéologie orientale
RLA	Reallexikon der Assyriologie
RO	Rocznik Orientalistyczny
SGL	Sumerische Götterlieder
StBoT	Studien zu den Boğazköy-Texten
SVJAD	A. Riftin, *Starovavilonskije juridičeskije i administrativnyje dokumenty v sobranijach SSSR*, Moskva, Leningrad 1937
TAPS	Transactions of the American Philosophical Society
TCL	Textes cunéiformes du Louvre
TCS	Texts from Cuneiform Sources
TIM	Texts in the Iraq Museum
TJDB	E. Szlechter, *Tablettes juridiques de la première dynastie de Babylone, conservées au Musée d'Art et d'Histoire de Genève*, Paris 1985
TM	Tell Mardikh
UET	Ur Excavations. Texts
UF	Ugarit Forschungen
Umma III	F. Yildiz, T. Gomi, *Die Umma-Texte aus den Archäologischen Museen zu Istanbul*, Bd. III (Nr. 1601-2300), Bethesda 1993
UVB	Vorläufiger Bericht über die... Ausgrabungen in Uruk-Warka, Berlin 1930ff.
VA	tablets in the collections of Vorderasiatische Museen zu Berlin
VAB	Vorderasiatische Bibliothek
VBoT	A. Götze, Verstreute Boghazköi-Texte
VS	Vorderasiatische Schriftdenkmäler der Königlichen Museen zu Berlin
YOS	Yale Oriental Series, Babylonian Texts
ZA	Zeitschrift für Assyriologie
ZATU	M. W. Green, H. J. Nissen, *Zeichenliste der archaischen Texte aus Uruk*, Berlin 1987

BIBLIOGRAPHY OF KRYSTYNA SZARZYŃSKA

1969 *Céramique d'Uruk d'après l'écriture pictographique sumérienne*, Études et Travaux II (Warsaw) 15-24.

1970 *Les plus anciennes inscriptions sur les tablettes d'Uruk*, Études et Travaux III (Warsaw) 5-15, 28 fig.

1971 *Literatura starożytnej Mezopotamii* [*The Literature of Ancient Mesopotamia*], in: J. Braun (ed.), *Mezopotamia* (Warsaw) 234-269.

1979 *Kosmogonia sumeryjska* [*Sumerian Cosmogony*], Euhemer – Przegląd Religioznawczy (Warsaw) 111, 41-54 [Engl. Summary].

1980 NAM_2:HUB_2 – *Sumerian Official in the Archaic Period*, RO 41, 125-130.

1981 *Some Remarks on the so-called „Steingebäude" in Archaic Uruk-Warka*, Akkadica 23, 45-49.

– with Krystyna Łyczkowska – *Mitologia Mezopotamii* [*Mesopotamian Mythology*] (Warsaw) 327 pp.

1983 *The Temple* é-dùg-nun/é-nun-dùg *in the Archaic City of Uruk*, Études et Travaux XII, 9-12.

1987 *The Sumerian Goddess* I n a n a k u r, Orientalia Varsoviensia 1: *Papers on Asia Past and Present* (Warsaw) 7-14.

1988 *Kult bogini Inany w Uruk w okresie archaicznym* [*Cult of the Goddess Inana in Uruk in the Archaic Period*], Euhemer – Przegląd Religioznawczy (Warsaw) 148, 3-11 [Engl. Summary].

Records of Garments and Cloths in Archaic Uruk/Warka, AoF 15, 220-230.

1989 *Some of the Oldest Cult Symbols in Archaic Uruk*, JEOL 30, 3-21, 8 tabl.

1992 *Names of Temples in the Archaic Texts from Uruk*, ASJ 14, 269-287.

1993 *Offerings for the Goddess Inana in Archaic Uruk*, RA 87, 7-28, 4 tabl.

Archaic Sumerian Signs for Garments and Cloths, RO 48/2, 9-22 (1994).

Archaic Sumerian Signs Indicating Successive Days, ŠULMU IV: Papers Presented at the International Conference in Poznań, 19-22 September, 1989 (Poznań) 273-285.

1994 *Archaic Sumerian Tags*, JCS 46, 1-10.

1996 *Some Comments on Individual Entires in the* URUK-*Sign-List ZATU* [Review of M. W. Green - H. J. Nissen, *Zeichenliste der archaischen Texte aus Uruk*, 1987], ASJ 18, 235-242.

Sumer, in: K. Szarzyńska et al., *Miłość i seks w kulturach Wschodu Starożytnego* [*Love and Sex in the Cultures of the Ancient Near East*] (Warsaw) 7-44.

Epilogue in M. Bielicki, *Zapomniany świat Sumerów,* [Re-edition] (Warsaw) 349-351.

1997 *Sumerica. Prace sumeroznawcze* [Re-edition of some earlier publications, with *Introduction*] (Warsaw).

Cult of the Goddess Inana in Archaic Uruk, in: *Sumerica* (see above), 141-153.

In press:

Archaic Sumerian Standards, JCS 47.

THE STELE (NA-RÚ) IN THE EBLA DOCUMENTS

Alfonso Archi
Rome

1. J.-M. Durand has noted that, in the entry KUR.PAD na-rú = *ma-da-ù zi-ga-na-tim* of the Lexical Lists (manuscript *C*), the second Eblaite word is *sikkannu* „stele, betyl"[1] (MEE IV, p. 216: 166a, 166b; [*B*] KUR.PAD na-rú = *ma-da-u₉* na₄-na₄; [*D*] KUR.PAD na-rú = *na-ša-du*).[2]

Mari had already provided an example of betyl for the third millennium from the area of the temple of Ninni-zaza. It has the shape of an elongated regular cone, 1.50 m high and with a base 35 cms in diameter. This betyl may originally have been placed in the centre of the temple courtyard.[3]

Ebla proves now that the term *sikkannu* was already attested in Syria in the third millennium.

Betyls have also been found in the Ebla temples of the 17th-16th centuries. In temple N, in the lower city, a basalt monolith was found leaning against two basalt slabs in the south-east corner. One side shows a small hole for pouring offerings. During the final phase of use of temple D, situated on the western slope of the acropolis, two betyls were erected near the back wall of the *cella*, behind an offerings table.[4]

Two aniconic stelae (*skn*) come from Ugarit. These were raised (as their inscriptions explain) for a funerary sacrifice (*pgr*) in honour of Dagan.[5]

Recently, the epigraphic documentation for Syria of the 2nd millennium has been increased. Three letters from Mari tell us of orders given to craftsmen for the preparation of three betyls (*sikkannu*), respectively for Ištar, Dagan and

---

[1] J.-M. Durand, NABU 1988, 8, pp. 5-6.

[2] For the interpretation of the glosses (*ns^c*; **mtH*), „removal of the stelae", see G. Conti, *Miscellanea Eblaitica* 3 (QuSem 17, Firenze 1990) p. 91. In the Pre-Sargonic examples where PAD means „to tear out" its reading is apparently bur_x, see PSD B, p. 165b under 6, ḫé-bur_x (PAD)-re_6-ne = *li-su-ḫa*, Rim C 9:31 (courtesy of P. Steinkeller).

[3] A. Parrot, *Les temples d'Ishtarat et de Ninni-zaza* (Paris 1967) pp. 25-26.

[4] P. Matthiae, *Ebla. Un impero ritrovato* (Torino 1977) pp. 130-131, 138, and tables 64-65, 68-69; see further note 19.

[5] M. Yon - P. Bordreuil - D. Pardee, in M. Yon (ed.), *Arts et industries de la pierre* (Ras Shamra-Ougarit VI, Paris 1991) pp. 301-303.

Haddu.[6] Moreover, ARMT XXIII 284 records the sacrifice of a sheep for the betyl of Dagan. The texts of Emar show that a *sikkannu* was dedicated to each of the two principal gods, Ninurta and Ḫebat.[7] Further, in the *zukru* festival certain gods were carried out from the temple and received sacrifices of animals and offerings in front of the betyls, which were then anointed with fat and oil, Emar VI/3: 373 ll. 22-32, 43-58 (in ll. 185-189 the chariot of Dagan was made to pass between two betyls).[8]

These new data have provoked renewed interest in exploring meanings and functions of the betyls in the cults of Syria and Palestine.[9]

The epigraphic data of Ebla, however, requires some explanation.

2. The bilingual Lexical Lists present another entry with na-rú, that is na-rú = *maš-ar-tum* / *maš-ar-du-um* (MEE IV, p. 300: 899).[10] While the Sumerian term appears several times (although not frequently) in the administrative documents, at the moment I am able to quote only the following three passages for the Eblaite one.

{1} TM.75.G.1796 (MEE X 4) rev. II 6-9:] 6 g[ín DILMUN] kù-gi nu_{11}-za 1 an-dùl *maš-ar-tum Ib-rí-um* „] 6 shekels of gold (for) covering 1 statue (of) the stele of Ibrium".

[6] Durand, *Le culte des bétyles en Syrie*, in J.-M. Durand - J.-R. Kupper (eds.), *Miscellanea Babylonica. Mélanges offerts à M. Birot* (Paris 1985) pp. 79-84.

[7] D.E. Fleming, *The Installation of Baal's High priestess at Emar* (Atlanta 1992) pp. 75-79. The administrative documents of Emar have been published by D. Arnaud, *Recherches au pays d'Aštata.* Emar VI/1 (Paris 1985); Emar VI/3 (Paris 1986). The documentation from Tall Munbāqa seem to point to an use of the *sikkannu* in the cult of the dead, see M. Dietrich - O. Loretz - W. Mayer, *Sikkanum 'Betyle'*, UF 21 (1989) pp. 133-139; cf. below, section 8.

[8] In Hittite Anatolia a widespread renewal cult foresaw that the image of the god be taken, each year, to its own stele outside the city, see Archi, *Fêtes de printemps et d'autonne et réintégration rituelle d'images de culte dans l'Anatolie hittite*, UF 5 (1973) 7-27.

[9] M. Hutter, *Kultstelen und Baityloi*, in B. Janowski - K. Koch - G. Wilhelm (eds.), *Religionsgeschichtliche Beziehungen zwischen Kleinasien, Nordsyrien und dem Alten Testament* (Freiburg 1993) pp. 87-108; T. N. D. Mettinger, *No Grave Image? Israelite Aniconism in its Ancient Near Eastern Context*, (Stockholm 1995); J. C. de Moor, *Standing Stones and Ancestor Worship*, UF 27 (1995) pp. 1-20.

[10] In the Word List TM.75.G.1822+, dupl. 10011+, new fragments allow to read in l. 90: na-ERIN. M. Civil, in L. Cagni (ed.), *Ebla 1975-1985* (Napoli 1987) pp. 144 and 156, had suggested to restore [na-rú-a] basing himself on *na-a-rí* of the Semitic version of that list, TM.75.G.1316.

In ARET I, p. 298, the present writer had interpreted the Eblaite gloss as Akk. *māšartu* „muster, inspection", an explanation which cannot be accepted. If *mašartu* derives from *š'r, Akk. *ša'āru* „to be victorious, to win", Ar. *ṯġr* „to smash", we get *mašārtu* „stele for a victory"; this cannot be, however, the primary meaning in the Eblaite documentation.

In Emar a *mašartu* priestess (^{SAL}*maš-ar-tu*$_4$) of Ištar is known, and *Emar* VI/3 370 is the ritual for the priestess's installation. According to D. Fleming, in M.W. Chavals (ed.), *Emar: The History, Religion, and Culture of a Syrian Town in the Late Bronze Age* (Bethesda 1996) p. 91, the priestess's title may also derive from *ša'āru*; the principal feasting participants of the ritual are the LÚ^{meš} *ta-ḫa-zi* „battle personnel", see ll. 32, 62, 65, 68, 90.

{2} TM.75.G.10210 obv. XIV 20-23: (geštu$_x$-lá, šu-dub, GIŠ-DU) *Ti-bù-da-mu maš-ar-tum* en „(jewels to) Tibu-Damu (for / on the occasion of) the stele of the king".

{3} TM.75.G.10210 obv. XIV 23-XV 8: 3 gín DILMUN an-na [...] 1 GIŠ-ASAR ... 2 gín DILMUN kù-gi *'a$_5$(NI)-na-gu* 1 GIŠ-ASAR *maš-ar-tum* en „3 shekels of tin (for) [... of (?)] a plate ... 2 shekels of gold (for) the rim of a plate (for) the stele of the king".

3. In passage (1) it would appear that the stele was decorated with an image. That the stele may have been provided with a kind of plate or tray is confirmed by the following passage, the only one to my knowledge where a na-rú is connected to a god.

{4} ARET III 440 rev. IX 1-4: 1 1/2 gín DILMUN bar$_6$:kù GIŠ-ASAR na-rú ^{d}*'À-da* „1,5 shekels of silver (for) a plate (for) the stele of Hadda".

The stele may also have had a table.

{5} TM.75.2428 rev. XIII 18-24: 1 1/2 kù-gi maš-maš 1 GIŠ-banšur *Nu-ba-du* dumu-mí *Ù-ti* na-rú en „1,5 shekels of gold (for)... 1 table (to) Nubatu, the daughter of Uti (son of the vizier Ibrium), (for) the stele of the king".

A small amount of silver, 78 gr, is destined for a stele also in the following passage.

{6} ARET II 6 (22): 10 gín DILMUN bar$_6$:kù na-rú.

4. In the administrative documents, with the exception of passage {4} mentioning the stele of the weather-god Hadda, na-rú „erected stone, stele"[11] is always connected with the king, the viziers Ibrium and Ibbi-Zikir or other persons. „On the day / on the occasion of the festivity of their stele", *in* ud ḫúl na-rú-*sù*, these people received gifts or, according to some mu-DU texts, made offerings.

Stele of the king: {2}, {3}, {5}.

Stele of the vizier Ibrium: {1} and the three following passages.

{7} ARET III 274+ obv. II 2-8: *Ib-rí-um* en šu-mu-"tag$_4$" *in* ud ḫúl na-rú[-*sù*] „(gifts for) Ibrium the king has brought on the day of [his] festival".

{8} TM.75.G.1705 rev. IV 7-10: *Ib-rí-um in* ud ḫúl na-rú[-*sù*] „(gifts for) Ibrium on the day of the festival of [his] stele".

Stele of Ibbi-Zikir, who succeeded his father Ibrium as vizier.

[11] For na-rú(-a) in inscriptions of the Early Dynastic period, see H. Behrens - H. Steible, *Glossar zu den Altsumerischen Bau- und Weihinschriften* (FAOS 6, Freiburg 1983) pp. 242-243. For *narû* and its possible meaning in Old Babylonian, see J.G. Westenholz, in *kinattūtu ša dārâti. R. Kutscher Memorial Volume* (Tel Aviv 1993) pp. 205-218.

{9} TM.75.G.1527 rev. VI 3-10: mu-DU *I-bí-zi-kir* dumu-nita *Ib-rí-um in* ud ḫúl na-rú-*sù* šu-ba$_4$-ti „(gifts,) delivery (which) Ibbi-Zikir, son of Ibrium, has received on the day of the festival of his stele".

Stelae of other officials:

{10} MEE II 25 obv. V 6-12: *A*-KA-*ma in* ud ḫúl na-rú-*sù Ìr-am*$_6$*-da-mu* šu-mu-"tag$_4$" „(clothes for 'lord', lugal) AKAma on the day of the festival of his stele, Iram-Damu has brought".

{11} ARET III 468 obv. IX 1-4:] *'À-téš in* ud ḫúl na-rú-*sù* „] (for 'lord', lugal,) Ateš on the day of the festival of his stele".

{12} TM.75.G.1459 obv. VIII 5-IX 2: mu-DU *En-na*-BAD *in* ud na-rú-*sù* „(objects,) delivery (of 'lord', lugal,) Enna-BAD on the day of the festival of his stele".

{13} TM.75.G.2031 rev. VII 6-14: *Ḫa-ra-il* ì-na-sum níg-ba en *in Šè-'à-am*^{ki} *in* ud ḫúl na-rú-*sù* „(objects which 'lord', lugal,) Ḫarail has given (as) a gift (for) the king in the town of Š. on the day of the festival of his stele".

{14} ARET III 669 I 2-8: lú mu-DU *Ib-rí-um* ì-na-sum *Puzur*$_4$*-ra-ḫa-al*$_6$ *in* ud ḫúl na-rú-*sù* „(objects) which (are) the delivery Ibrium has given (to 'lord', lugal,) Puzurra-ḫa'al on the day of the festival of his stele".

{15} ARET III 872 III 2-5: *A-šum in* ud ḫúl na-rú-*sù* „(clothes for)] Ašum on the day of the festival of his stele".

{16} TM.75.G.4578+4584 rev. III 4-7: *Ar-ra-ḫi-iš in* ud ḫúl na-rú-*sù* „(clothes to) Arraḫiš on the day of the festival of his stele".

{17} TM.75.G.4125+4131+4132 I 1-6:] *A-šum in* ud ḫúl na-rú-*sù Za-ba-rúm* šu-mu-"tag$_4$" „clothes (to)] Ašum on the day of the festival of his stele Zaburum has brought".

{18} ARET I 14 (15): *A-zi-za* lú *A-lum in* ud GIŠ.DUG.DU en *si-in* ḫúl na-rú-*sù* „(clothes to) Aziza of Alum when ... the king for the festival of his stele".

{19} TM.75.G.2464 rev. VII 9-15: *Ba-lu*-KA ur$_4$ *Ì-mar*^{ki} *in* ud ḫúl na-rú-*sù* KA-*ba-lum* šu-mu-"tag$_4$" „(1 mina of silver for 1 belt 1 scabbard 1 curved dagger for) BaluKA, the official ur$_4$ of Emar, on the day of the festival of his stele KAbalum has brought".

5. The second formula in which na-rú appears is: nídba na-rú „offering (for) the stele".

{20} MEE II 14 (mu-DU text; before the period of vizier Ibrium) rev. IX 4-6: dub nídba na-rú „(Total: 108+61 clothes delivered by three dozens 'lords', lugal.) Tablet (concerning) the offering (for) the stele".

{21} MEE II 48 rev. IX 2-VIII 2: dub-gar lú níg-ba dingir-dingir-dingir-dingir *áš-du* nídba na-rú 7 mu 6 mu 5 mu 4 mu 3 mu 2 mu „([Total: 94] minas 58 shekels of silver.) Document of the gifts (for) the gods by (/ concerning) the offering (for) the stele, (for the) 7th year, 6th year, 5th year, 4th year, 3rd year, 2nd year".

{22} TM.75.G.4512 (mu-DU text; before the period of vizier Ibrium) rev. III 1-4:] mu-DU nídba na-rú 7 mu „] delivery (for) the offering (for) the stele; 7th year".

{23} ARET I 31 (mu-DU text registering the deliveries of four foreign kings and three officials) (8): dub na-rú „(Total: 16+5 clothes.) Tablet of (the offering of ?) the stele".

References to the festival of the stele is made in two deliveries of clothes.

{24} ARET IV 16 (49): *A-da-mu En-ar-li-im* šu-mu-"tag$_4$" *in* ud nídba na-rú „(clothes to) Adamu, Enar-Lim has brought on the day of the offering (for) the stele".

{25} ARET III 31 obv. VI 1-4:] lú *Iš-da-maḫ in* ud nídba na-rú „] which (is for) Išdamaḫ on the day of the offering (for) the stele".

6. MEE II 45, dated to the earliest phase of the archives, refers to the decoration of a stele. The first part of the document records small amounts of metals which seem to be left over from other works, for example obv. I 1-3: 10 gín DILMUN kù-gi „tag$_4$" 1 íb-lá *si-ti-tum* gír-kun 1 ma-na kù-gi „10 shekels of gold: remains (from the working of) 1 belt (with) scabbard (and) curved dagger of 1 mina of gold". The total quantity of metals is 10 shekels of gold, 10 of silver, 6 of bronze, 4 of copper as well as 1 mina of copper given by Igriš-Ḫalab, the third from last king of Ebla (obv. V 3-rev. I 4). The total, 1 and a half mina, is of 705 grams. The final part of the document would appear to read as follows:

{26} MEE II 45 obv. V 3-rev. II 5: 1 ma-na a-gar$_5$-gar$_5$ *Ig-rí-iš-Ḫa-lab*$_x$ en *Ib-la*^{ki} na-rú *in* DIŠ mu DU *Tar*$_5$*-kab-du-lum 'a*$_5$*-na Kak-mi-um*^{ki} simug-simug na-rú „(10+10+4+2+4 shekels,) 1 mina of copper (of) Igriš-Ḫalab, king of Ebla, (for) the stele. In the year of the going of Tarkab-dulum to Kakmium. (To) the smiths (for doing) the stele".

A date according to the „year of the offering (for) the stele of Igriš-Ḫalab [x (?) of Eb]la" is found in a poorly preserved small tablet which contains a very short letter of „Irkab-damu king of Ebla", ([*en-ma Ìr-*]*kab*-[*da-*]*mu* en *Ib-la*^{ki}), the successor of Igriš-Ḫalab:

{27} TM.75.G.12497 rev. II 2-III 1: DIŠ mu nídba na-⌜rú⌝ *Ig-rí-iš-Ḫa-lab*$_x$ [x(?) *Ib-*]*la*^{ki}

7. na-rú appears in the plural in only one passage:

{28} *ARET* III 99 I 4-9: maškim NE-*zi-ma-lik* níg-AN.AN.AN.AN *Ib-rí-um* na-rú-na-rú [x]-DU [„(1+1+1 clothes for) the agent of NEzi-malik (for) the ... (of) Ibrium (for) the stelae ..."

8. The Lexical List *B* (quoted in 1.) has na_4-na_4, that is „stones", instead of *sikkannātim*. Passages {6} and {26} show, however, that the na-rú stelae of Ebla were decorated with metal, and metal objects were used for their cult, see {3}-{5}.

Most of these stelae were, perhaps aniconic, but that of the vizier Ibrium ({1}) was carved, or at least had an image on it.

According to passage {4}, one na-rú was dedicated to a god, Hadda. It is possible that this stele was similar to and had the same function as that of the temple of Ninni-zaza at Mari. This is, however, the only case: all the other passages relate the na-rú to men.[12]

It has been attempted to show how, for Ugarit at least, the betyls belonged to the cult of the dead.[13] The *sikkannu* is certainly a symbol of death in the curse which closes certain contracts from Tall Munbāqa[14] and Emar, see *Emar* VI/3. 125 ll. 35-41: „Whoever changes these words (of the contract), may Dagan, Ninurta and Išḫara destroy his descendants and his name! May a stele be erected on his house (^{na_4}*sí-kà-na a-na* é-*šu li-iz-qú-up*)!" (see also 17, ll. 32-40).

At Ebla, as at Emar, besides the stelae of gods there were the stelae of men. However, when a stele was celebrated (ḫúl) at Ebla, the person to whom it belonged was without doubt alive. Perhaps the celebration of the stele marked the assumption of a role, of an office.[15] This calls to mind the stelae at Assur of the kings and the officials of the middle Assyrian period, which stood on the south side of the city facing the inner city wall.[16] However, these officials of Ebla, the "lords", lugal, were clearly not eponyms; they formed a group of 14–20 individuals who had administrative responsibilities.[17]

[12] See however si-dù, below, section 9.

[13] de Moor, UF 27 (1995) pp. 1-20.

[14] See Dietrich - Loretz - Mayer, UF 21 (1989), pp. 136-137.

[15] G. Pettinato, MEE II, pp. 52 and 308, has already suggested that the festival of the stele was related to „the beginning of an *Amtsperiode* of both the sovereign and a high official". He maintains that the number or name of year in which the event occurred was carved on the stelae (this latter hypothesis can be excluded).

[16] For these stelae, see J. V. Canby, Iraq 38 (1976), pp. 121-125.

[17] Here we should consider the stelae of Tell Chuera, to be date to the middle of the 3rd millennium and, therefore, chronologically very close to the epigraphic documentation of Ebla. This is what W. Orthmann, *Tell Chuera* (Damaskus-Tartous 1990) p. 24, writes on these stelae: „Östlich der eigentlichen

This interpretation, however, raises certain problems. The stele of Igriš-Ḫalab, the third from last king, occurs in {26} and {27}. There is, instead, no explicit mention of the stele of Irkab-Damu. The na-rú en of {2}-{3} and {5} was that of the last king, Išar-Damu, since the first text is dated to the time of the vizier Ibrium and the second to Ibbi-Zikir.[18] We do not know where the stelae of the kings were erected.[19] According to a single text, {21}, these received annual offerings (nídba). When text {26} was written, Igriš-Ḫalab had already been king for some time. If a stele was really erected in his honour at the start of his reign, then we must accept that, later, the smiths received quantities of metal for its embellishment.

As far as the viziers are concerned, No. {8} is an annual account of silver distributed by the Palace which presents various archaic forms and has, therefore, been dated to the first year of the mandate of Ibrium.[20] Since this tablet does not begin with the formula normally found in this kind of document („1 mina of silver for the head in silver of the god Kura"), it must have been preceded by another tablet from the same year which could be text {7}. The celebration of the stele of Ibbi-Zikir, son and successor of Ibrium, is mentioned in

Stadtanlage hatte schon M. v. Oppenheim eine Anzahl großer, teils aufrecht stehender, teils umgestürzter Steinplatten beobachtet, die in zwei Reihen zu beiden Seiten einer 'Straße' aufgestellt sind. Diese 'Straße' verläuft ungefähr in Nord-Süd-Richtung, sie ist mehrere Meter breit. Über dem gewachsenen Boden findet sich eine dünne Schotterschicht, die vielleicht eine Art Straßenbelag darstellt. Die Steinplatten, von denen heute nur noch zwei aufrecht stehen, waren anscheinend nicht in regelmäßigen Abständen aufgestellt. Viele sind zerbrochen, vielleicht auch zerschlagen worden, um als Baumaterial zu dienen. Die unten dreieckig spitz zugeschlagenen Platten waren in Gruben gesetzt und mit größeren Steinen verkeilt worden. Für die ganze Anlage gibt es im syrisch-mesopotamischen Raum keine Parallelen, so daß eine Deutung bisher nicht möglich ist. Untersuchungen in der Umgebung der Stelenstraße haben bisher keinen Anhaltspunkt dafür erbracht, daß dieser Bereich etwa als Friedhof gedient haben könnten."

[18] See Archi, *Amurru* I (1996), pp. 78 and 80.

[19] In the levels above Hypogeum G4, in the northern area of Palace G (preliminary notes in Matthiae, CRAIB 1995, pp. 655-659) a basalt monolith (unpublished) was found in a disturbed context erected within a circle of stones. This stood in Ec V8 ii+iii/Ec V7 i+iv, 5 metres to the west of the western wall of the hypogeum; it is aligned with the norther wall. Its base lies on a level about 1 metre above the preserved top of the northern wall of the hypogeum. The monolith is in the shape of an elongated, irregular cone, and its surface is polished. The less than perfect working of the stone suggests a date in the Amorite period.

The hypogeum consisted of two rooms of roughly 4 x 5 metres. The building of the Royal Palace G must have been begun by Irkab-Damu. Išar-Damu may have completed it, probably extending the building and certainly making several changes. The hypogeum is situated 6 metres below the floor of the latest reworking of the sector, in the heart of the Palace. It is plausible that such a monumental structure was planned during the building phase of the Palace. However, the fact that not even one fragment of pottery has been found in the two rooms makes one suspect that the hypogeum was never used. In several accounts concerning distributions of bread, the king, en, is followed by „the kings", en-en, perhaps „the (dead) kings", ARET IX obv. I 5-6; 14 obv. I 4-6; 26 rev. II 2-3, III 2-3, etc., see p. 384. This fact seems to prove that the king's ancestors received regular offerings at the Palace.

[20] See Archi, *Amurru* I (1996), p. 76.

{9}. This is an annual account of deliveries to the Palace by the vizier and „lords". This is certainly one of the last annual mu-DU texts of Ibrium, but precedes, however, MEE II 1, which opens with the deliveries of Ibrium and then records his death. So, if we want to suggest that a stele was erected at the start of a mandate, we must suppose that Ibbi-Zikir was made vizier when his father, possibly in failing health, was still alive.

Mentions of the festival (ḫúl) of the stele are few with respect to the number of „lords", lugal, and they ({10}-{14}) concern mainly texts to be dated before Ibrium. Is the fact that, with Ibrium, the power of the „lords" began to decline a sufficient reason to explain this situation? The texts can be dated only approximately, but it is possible that in those cases the celebration of the stele indicates the assuming of their position by the lords. In the mu-DU texts {12} and {13} the two lords deliver goods on the occasion of the celebration of their stelae, as though in exchange for the honour bestowed on them.

Letter {27} is dated to the „year of the offering (for) the stele of Igriš-Ḫalab [of Eb]la", when the king was already Irkab-damu. Is this possibly an offering for the death of Igriš-Ḫalab? It is likely that also in passages {20}-{25} the offerings (nídba) were for the stele of the king (and not that of Hadda).

Text {21} records the gifts made to various gods on the occasion of offerings to the stele, from the 2nd to the 7th years. We have no indication that a cultic cycle of seven years existed at Ebla. Therefore, numbering of this kind only has sense if referred to the period of a king's reign. Since in obv. VIII 1 the dam dingir priestess Tirin-Damu is mentioned (she died halfway through the reign of Išar-Damu, the last king, when two younger dam dingir priestesses were already active),[21] the seven years refer probably to the period of Irkab-Damu's reign. Document {20} contains the list of clothes given as a gift by the principal officials of the reign on the occasion of one of these annual offerings. This document is also to be dated (according to the personal names mentioned therein) to the first years of Irkab-Damu, if not to the last of Igriš-Ḫalab. Text {23}, a later one, records instead the gifts of four foreign kings and of three officials.

It would appear that only the weather-god Haddu had a stele (No. {14}). The other gods were represented only by statues (an-dùl). It is, therefore, certain that at Ebla the aniconic cult was absolutely secondary, although some cults were probably centred on stelae and betyls, as at Mari and Emar (see 9.).

[21] See Archi, *Festschrift O. Loretz*, in press.

9. The term si-dù has been explained as „the horn-shaped parts of an altar" by J. G. Dercksen.[22] This interpretation was accepted by M.G. Biga commenting TM.75.G.1730 rev. IX 22-28: 1 uš:bar lú tuš 2 si-dù en *wa ma-lik-tum* „(silver for) 1 stick, which (has to) stay (for) the 2 si-dù of the king and of the queen". She noted that si-dù must be an object since the stick belongs to it.[23] The Lexical Lists have the entry si-dù = *ti-mu-mu* (MEE IV, p. 320: 1116). At first, G. Pettinato explained *ti-mu-mu* with **dmm* „to lament", and si-dù was „lamentation".[24] Recently, however, he takes this term to mean „stone, stele", linking it with the Heb. *d^{e}mûth*.[25]

The documentation should be ordered as follows:[26]

1) *da-mu/mi, da-mi-mu, da-a-mu*. The contexts suggest „one who laments", from **dmm*;

2) *da-ma-ti*. It is linked to ki-sur, cfr. Akk. *kisurrû* „boundary (stone, *kudurru*), territory". See ARET I 13 (7): *in da-ma-ti* ki-sur; TM.75.G.10074 obv. X 23-24: *da-ma-ti-iš* ki-sur GN_1 *wa* GN_2. Here the meaning „boundary stone" would seem to apply;

3) a parallel passage with si-dù is TM.75.G.2238 obv. XII 21-24: 1 udu ki-sur si-dù-si-dù en-en. See further TM.75.G.2238 obv. IV 21-23: 20 udu si-dù-si-dù en-en; TM.75.G.1765 rev. III 1-2: si-dù-si-dù en-en; TM.75.G.1730 rev. IX 25-28: 2 si-dù en *wa ma-lik-tum*. In the ritual for the royal marriage, *ARET* XI 1-2, si-dù is linked to both the king and the queen; 1 (77), 2 (81): si-dù en ...([si-dù]) *ma-lik-tum*; and also to the god Kura; 1 (13) and 2 (16): 2 si-dù ^{d}*Ku-ra*.

There are, therefore, elements to enable us to state that si-dù / *damâtum* is, in effect, a kind of „erected betyl" in the shape of a cone (si) that is ending in a point. This served as a boundary stone.[27] These betyls played an important role in the funerary cult: si-dù-si-dù en-en were the betyls of the dead kings, before which sheep (udu) were sacrificed. In the marriage ritual ARET XI 1-2 (cfr. TM.75.G.1730), however, we find also a betyl of the king and another of the queen, and two for Kura, that is to say for Kura and his consort Barama.

Amongst the offerings to the gods, instead, bull horns (si) are frequent, above all in offerings to Hadda of Ḫalab, but also to other gods such as Aštabil

[22] J. G. Dercksen, NABU 1989, 39, pp. 26-27.

[23] M. G. Biga, Vicino Oriente 8/2 (1992) pp. 8-9.

[24] Pettinato, OA 18 (1979), p. 115. This interpretation has been accepted by P. Fronzaroli, *ARET* XI, p. 167.

[25] Pettinato, *Il rituale per la successione al trono di Ebla* Roma 1992 [but 1993] p. 201.

[26] See already Archi, Vicino Oriente 10 (1996), pp. 46-48 note 19, for a more detailed presentation of the documentation.

[27] Notwithstanding the doubts expressed by the present writer, op. cit., p. 48 note 19.

and Rašap. These horns were always offered in pairs: 2 si gud / si-si 2 gud „two horns of a bull / the horns of 4 bulls".[28]

Addendum

The stelae of three other „lords", lugal, of the period preceding the vizier Ibrium are mentioned:

{29} TM.76.G.882 obv. I 1-II 1: 2 *mi-at* 60 ma-na babbar:kù 41 GIŠ-sú mu-DU *Ti-ir in* ud [ḫu]l na-rú<-sù> „260 minas of silver, 41 seats: delivery of Tir on the occasion of the festivity of (his) stele." Tir was, together with Darmia, the most important lugal before Arrukum became vizier.[29]

{30} TM.75.G.10276 (the vizier was Arrukum) rev. X 1-4: túg-NI.NI na-rú *Du-bí-šum* lú *Sá-gu-si*.

{31} TM.75.G.10276 rev. XI 4-6: (clothes) *Ar-si-a-ḫa in* ud na-rú.

P. Steinkeller has shown the identity between dù and rú (as in na-rú-a = *na-ru-ú*); the verb is /dru/ „to build" (*banû*, *epēšu*), „to erect" (*zaqāpu*), „to fasten" (*retû*).[30]

For na$_4$ „stone" with the meaning „stele",[31] see also TM.75.G.2588 obv. III 7-10: (PN) šeš-II-ib dag$_x$ (LAK 457) 2 na$_4$ en.

[28] ARET III, p. 382.
[29] A. Archi, Amurru 1 (1996) pp. 19-20.
[30] P. Steinkeller, JCS 35 (1983) 249-250.
[31] See above, section 8.

THE TURBANED STANDARD OF IŠTAR*

Paul-Alain Beaulieu
Harvard University

Standards as symbols of the divine or royal presence have recently been the subject of a study in which both the iconographic and the literary evidence are discussed.[1] In Neo-Assyrian art such standards are depicted on both seals and monumental reliefs. They consist typically of a pole topped with a circular openwork decorative piece from which hang a pair of tassels. There are some textual references to such standards. In Neo-Babylonian texts from Uruk divine standards designated by the word *urigallu* are mentioned a few times. There was an *urigallu* of the goddess Ištar and one of the goddess Uṣur-amāssu. The word also appears in connection with no specific deity, and it is always preceded by the divine determinative. The divine character of the *urigallu* is also underscored by its mention, alongside various deities, in one text which appears to be an offering list (ARRIM 7, 47: 17. ^{d}*ùri-gal-*[*lum*]). References to the deified standards of the two goddesses are as follows:

YOS 17, 245: 1. 8½ GÍN *gi-ru-u* KÙ.GI 2. 1-*en da-áš-šú* KÙ.GI *šá* ^{d}⌈*ùri*⌉-*gal-lum* 3. *šá* ^{d}INNIN UNUG^{ki} 4. ^{I}*ri-mut* A-*šú šá* ^{Id}EN-ŠEŠ-MU 5. ^{lú}KÙ.DIM IGI-*er*

„Eight and one twelfth shekels of gold (for) one golden *daššu* belonging to the divine standard of Ištar-of-Uruk, received by Rīmūt, son of Bēl-aḫ-iddin, the goldsmith".

YOS 7, 183: 32. 2 MA.NA TÚG *mi-iḫ-ṣi šá* SÍG ḪÉ.ME.DA *šá in-za-ḫu-re-*⌈*e*⌉*-ti* 1 TÚG *par-ši-gu šá* ^{d}*ùri-gal-lum* 33. šá ^{d}GAŠAN šá UNUG^{ki} 34. 1 2/3 MA.NA KI.MIN *šá* ^{d}*ùri-gal-lum šá* ^{d}ÙRI-INIM-*su*

„Two minas of woven cloth of red-colored wool (dyed) with *inzaḫurētu* (for) one turban for the divine standard of the Lady-of-Uruk; one and two-third minas of the same for the divine standard of Uṣur-amāssu",

---

* When P. Steinkeller's contribution to this volume was already in the hands of the editors, Dr. Paul-Alain Beaulieu provided him with information that has important bearing on the topic of his article. In view of the significance of this information, Steinkeller invited Dr. Beaulieu to present it in a separate communication. P.S.

[1] B. Pongratz-Leisten, K. Deller and E. Bleibtreu, *Götterstreitwagen und Götterstandarten: Götter auf dem Feldzug und ihr Kult im Feldlager*, BaghMitt 23 (1992) 291-356, especially B. Pongratz-Leisten, *Mesopotamische Standarte in Literarischen Zeugnissen*, BaghMitt 23 (1992) 299-340.

PTS 2282: 18. 1 *par-ši-gu šá* ^{d}*ùri-gal-lum šá* ^{d}GAŠAN šá UNUG^{ki}; 23. 1 *par-ši-gu šá* ^{d}*ùri-gal-lum šá* ^{d}ÙRI-INIM-*su*

„One turban (of red-colored wool dyed with *inzaḫurētu*) for the divine standard of the Lady-of-Uruk; one turban (of red-colored wool dyed with *inzaḫurētu*) for the divine standard of Uṣur-amāssu".[2]

NCBT 625: 2. [d]⌈*ùri*⌉*-gal-lum* 3. [*šá*] ^{d}⌈ÙRI-*a-mat*⌉*-su* (in very damaged context).

These texts are quite informative since they describe decorative pieces belonging to the standards. As noted by Pongratz-Leisten, the term *paršigu* must certainly denote in this context the tassels or streamers which are depicted hanging from the top portions of the *urigallu*s in Neo-Assyrian art.[3] While she does not propose an interpretation of the word *daššu* in YOS 17, 245, I would speculate that this might be identical with the word *daššu* which normally refers to an animal,[4] possibly a buck. Horned animals in jumping posture are depicted in the decorative pieces of openwork which top several of the standards depicted in late iconography.[5]

These references strongly support Steinkeller's proposal that the archaic emblem (urin\ÙRI, later *urigallu*) of the goddess Inanna was a scarf or turban (bar-si, *paršigu* in late texts) attached to the top of a pole.[6] Literary references to scarves of lapis lazuli seem to indicate blue-colored fabric, while Neo-Babylonian references mention red-colored ones (*inzaḫurētu*). This, however, is a minor detail considering the enormous time distance between the archaic and Neo-Babylonian evidence. Another difference appears to be the circular head of the pole, which in the archaic period may have been meant to depict the loop formed by the bar-si, while in the late periods this was replaced by a circular band of metalwork at the base of which the *paršigu* was probably tied. Otherwise the survival of a nearly identical cultic symbol for the same goddess in the same city provides one more example of the remarkable continuity of Mesopotamian civilization across the three millennia of its documented existence.

---

[2] This occurs in a list of ten paršigus for which are disbursed, line 15: 9 1/3 MA.NA *mi-iḫ-ṣi šá* SÍG ḪÉ.ME.DA *šá in-za-ḫu-re-e-tú*.

[3] BaghMitt 23 (1992) 329: „Diese Stoffe sind mit Sicherheit als die Troddeln oder Bänder der Standarten zu verstehen, wie sie auf den neuassyrischen Reliefs und Rollsiegeln abgebildet sind".

[4] CAD lists two words daššu. The first, daššu A „buck," is attested in lexical texts and šaziga prayers. The second, daššu B „a small metal implement," is attested in Neo-Babylonian archival texts but not in lexicography. Therefore it is possible that the word daššu in YOS 17, 245 refers to such an implement.

[5] See E. Bleibtreu, *Standarten auf neuassyrischen Reliefs und Bronzetreibarbeiten*, BaghMitt 23 (1992) 347-56, and especially tables 51-53.

[6] See pp. 87-100 in this volume.

FAÇON DE PARLER

Les expressions figées en droit mésopotamien

Henri Limet
Université de Liège

Une expression reste pur *flatus vocis*
tant qu'elle n'est pas corrélée,
en référence à un code donné,
à son contenu conventionné.

(Umberto Eco, *Lector in fabula*)

Les rédacteurs des actes juridiques, en Mésopotamie ancienne, étaient tenus de suivre des modèles formulaires[1]. Ils en dérogeaient peu et les façons de s'exprimer étaient coulées dans un moule *ne varietur*. Aussi n'est-on pas étonné de trouver un grand nombre d'expressions juridiques figées, parfois très imagées. Ces groupes de mots, étroitement soudés, doivent être considérés comme formant une unité et être employés tels quels dans les énoncés. Ils ont la particularité d'avoir souvent acquis par l'usage un sens différent de celui que leur donnent normalement leurs composants. Ces expressions „toutes faites" ne souffrent, ni l'insertion, ni la passivation, comme l'observe C. Hagège[2]; autrement dit le locuteur ou le scribe ne peuvent, ni ajouter un mot (un adjectif, par exemple), ni tourner à la forme passive une phrase active. D'autre part, elles ne prennent de sens que dans un contexte bien déterminé. Le lecteur de l'acte juridique sait qu'elles sont à interpréter ou à décoder „en droit"; comme le note Eco dans la citation rappelée plus haut, elles ont un contenu „par convention" et appartiennent à un ensemble de formules connues des juristes.

Toutes les expressions figées qui se rencontrent dans les textes juridiques ou dans d'autres écrits (des lettres, par exemple) qui traitent de telles questions, ne revèlent pas toutes du même tour d'esprit.

---

[1] Le présent article peut être considéré comme la suite de celui, intitulé *Vocabulaire technique du droit en sumérien*, paru dans M. E. Cohen et al. (éd.), *The Tablet and the Scroll* (in honor of W. W. Hallo), (Bethesda 1993) 140-145 et, plus lointainement, de *La formation du vocabulaire technique en sumérien* dans H. Klengel (éd.), *Gesellschaft und Kultur im alten Vorderasien* (Berlin 1982) 163-171.

[2] C. Hagège, *L'homme de paroles* (Paris 1985) 243. Hagège donne comme exemples en français: „casser sa pipe" (= mourir), „couper la poire en deux" (= faire des concessions réciproques). „Sa pipe est cassée ou „Une belle poire est coupée en deux" reprennent leur signification première.

1. Les lettrés babyloniens semblent avoir le goût des rencontres de mots, des allitérations, des assonances. Ils usent de formules dans lequelles des termes semblables, voire de même racine, se répondent[3]. A l'origine, il y a sans doute la tendance à apprécier les jeux de mots, sonores ou étymologiques, que favorisent les langues sémitiques, surtout grâce à la trilitéralité, et dont les Arabes usent de nos jours admirablement, dans le discours oral en particulier.

1.1. Un bon exemple nous est donné par Ai. 4, IV, 42-44: *bīta kima bīti-šu amēlu ana amēli išakkan* „l'un donnera à l'autre une maison pour une maison", ce qui correspond au sumérien é.a é.a.ni.gim lú.lú.ra in.gar.ra. Le sumérien lú.lú.ra a comme équivalent accadien *amēlu ana amēli* (Ai. 6, I, 18, 52,...) et lú.lú.a.g[im], *amēlu kima amēli* (Ai. 4, I, 62)[4]. On verra aussi (Ai. 6, II, 53): kù hé.a kù an.lá.e = *lu kaspu kaspa* [*išaqqal*] „si c'est de l'argent (à verser comme salaire), il payera en argent". Il n'est pas certain que l'expression sumérienne soit la langue originale, mais plutôt une traduction.

Dans les contrats de *tappûtum* qui associent deux agriculteurs pour prendre un champs en location, il est prévu qu'ils partageront la récolte à parts égales; auparavant: *awīlum mala awīlim manaḫtam išakkanu* „ils supporteront les frais l'un autant que l'autre"[5]. La rencontre des mots prend une valeur, non seulement esthétique, mais profonde si elle acquérait une efficacité certaine. C'est ce qui ressort d'une incantation:

[šu].ni in.ra	*qassu ilput-ma*	il a touché sa main,
[šu].ni.šè	*ana qāti-šu*	et sur sa main
im.mi.in.gar	*ištakan*	il l'a placée

Le texte se poursuit dans les mêmes termes avec le pied et la tête: „il a touché son pied... sa tête..."[6].

Le groupe *aḫum ana aḫim* est du même type (cf. CAD A/1, p. 203-204).

1.2. A Emar, relevons cette décision: *Ba'ala-bia al-ma-tu itti al-ma-na-ti ši-it a-zi-ib-tu it-ti az-ba-ti ši-it* „Ba'al-bia, elle sera veuve parmi les veuves, répudiée parmi les répudiées"[7].

---

[3] En français, l'expression „oeil pour oeil, dent pour dent", exprimant la célèbre loi du tallion, passe pour l'exemple type de style biblique.

[4] Cf. YOS 12, 190: šeš šeš-ra nu-mu-un-gi$_4$-gi$_4$; UET V, 205: šeš šeš-ra nu-ub-ta-bal. Une explication de ce style pourrait être à chercher dans la pauvreté du système pronominal, en particulier dans les pronoms indéfinis du type „l'un l'autre". On sait aussi que le petit nombre d'adjectifs qualificatifs a favorisé les tournures comme *aban šarruti* „une pierre de royauté" pour „une pierre royale" ou *al šarruti-ya* „la ville de ma royauté" pour „ma ville royale".

[5] L. de Kiere, *Old Babylonian real estate documents from Sippar* (Neuchâtel 1995) n° 495; 503: *manaḫta-šunu ippalu.*

[6] S. Lachenbacher, *Notes sur l'*ardat lili, RA 65 (1971) 146-147.

[7] Emar VI/3, n° 216, 11-12: „répudiée" ou „divorcée".

1.3. On notera l'emploi de l'accusatif dit „interne". Exemple: *bāqir ibaqqaru-šu*, mot à mot: le réclamant qui réclamerait contre lui[8]; suit alors la pénalité qui sanctionnerait celui qui, un jour, contesterait les stipulations du contrat. Autre formule du même genre et de même sens: *rāgim ragāmu*[9].

1.4. Une expression énigmatique: bar-nun bar-nun-šè! íb-ta-è (Ai 4, i, 46) a pour équivalent accadien: *ṣilipta ana ṣilipti ušeṣi* „il a loué (un terrain) la diagonale vers/sur la diagonale". Elle est laissée non traduite par CAD Ṣ, p. 188a, s.v. *ṣiliptu*, lex. Il faut sans doute la comprendre comme une allusion à une technique de labour que conseille le „Manuel d'agriculture" (les *Georgica* sumériennes): ki absin (APINxKUR) si-sá ì-uru$_4$-ru absin eškiri uru-ru-ab, ki absin eškiri ì-uru$_4$-ru, absin si-sá uru$_4$-ru-ab „l'endroit où tu as tracé des sillons droits, trace des sillons transversaux, l'endroit où tu as tracé des sillons transversaux, trace des sillons droits"[10]. Cela signifie qu'il faut labourer deux fois, une fois dans un sens („droit" = parallèlement à un côté du champ), une seconde fois, en recoupant perpendiculairement les premiers sillons.

2. Dans une deuxième catégorie, nous rangerons les syntagmes constitués d'éléments divers, qui indiquent, de façon concise, une clause particulière, mais fréquente, entre les parties de l'acte.

2.1. Le meilleur exemple est celui de *ṣimdat šarrim*, note qui termine souvent les contrats par lesquels un moissonneur est engagé et dont la forme plus développée mais incomplète est *kima ṣimdat šarrim*. On stipule ainsi qu'en cas d'absence, la sanction habituelle, telle qu'elle est énoncée par les décrets royaux, sera automatiquement appliquée. F. R. Kraus suppose que la simple mention de *ṣimdat šarrim* a pour but d'éviter les longues procédures ou les discussions interminables: la faute doit être punie sans délai ni tracasseries disproportionnées[11]. On notera aussi la tendance du droit, à l'époque, à rendre publiques des sanctions relevant du domaine privé; on dirait, en droit romain: à transformer en *crimen* un *delictum*.

2.2. Les Babyloniens, et ceux qui adoptèrent leur droit, se référaient aussi à des usages que chacun était censé connaître, d'où cette simple indication: *kima*

---

[8] ARM VIII, 1, 27; 4, 9; 8, 8...; TIM IV, 50. Les dictionnaires (CAD et AHw) préfèrent substituer /p/ au /b/ initial, d'où: *paqārum*.

[9] ARM VIII, 5, 8; voir ibid., p. 166, § 11, les commentaires de Boyer.

[10] Les deux versions prises en considération sont données par UET VI/2, 172, II, 17-18 et par OECT 1, pl. 32-35, W.-B. 170, III, 4-5. Pour la seconde, la copie porte ab-sín et ajoute systématiquement un /a/ devant /ab/, d'où uru$_4$-ru-a-ab.

[11] Exemple: *u$_4$ ebur-šè e-si-di i-la-ak, u-ul i-la-ak-ma ki-ma ṣi-im-da-at šarrim* „au jour de la moisson, il viendra moissonner; s'il ne vient pas, (ce sera) comme le décret du roi". YOS 13, 4 (*esidi* est remplacé par še-kin-kud); 55; 437. F. R. Kraus, RA 73 (1979) 51-62, voir les p. 60-61 § 9c. Voir déjà VAB V, p. 550.

ālim[12]. La série Ai 2, I, 34 et III, 32' montre bien que cette expression légale concerne l'intérêt d'un emprunt (máš uru-gim), le loyer d'un champ ou le cours du marché (ganba) tels qu'ils sont pratiqués habituellement „en ville" (uru gál-la = *ina āli ibašši*).

2.3. D'autres formules lapidaires sont très claires et leur utilité est aussi de remplacer de longs commentaires. C'est le cas de *ezib pî kunukki-šu* „mis à part la teneur du document (antérieur)". On la trouve dans les actes de prêt[13]. Sa signification est évidente: la présente reconnaissance de dette, que nous lisons, n'annule pas des dispositions figurant dans un acte précédent; éventuellement, deux emprunts se cumulent. Au point de vue linguistique, il est intéressant de voir que la formule complète s'abrège: l'adjectif *pānîm* „antérieur" est rarement écrit, de même le terme *pî* tombe parfois, ainsi que le montant de la dette première. On aboutit alors à un simple *ezib kunukku-šu*. Cette réduction de l'expression à l'essentiel montre bien qu'elle était bien comprise sans qu'il faille la développer en entier.

2.4. Dans les baux, la redevenance du locataire se calculera de la façon ainsi conçue: *ki-i-ma i-mi-tim ù šu-me-lim li-ib-ba ú-ṭà-ab* soit: „à gauche comme à droite il le satisfera"[14]. Le „code" de Hammourabi emploie cette expression et elle est fréquente à l'époque paléo-babylonienne. On entendait par là que le champ loué, qui était situé dans un terroir, devait rapporter au propriétaire ce que rapportaient les terrains voisins. Le terroir (a.gàr = *ugāru*) étant de productivité homogène et dépendant d'un système d'irrigation commun, il était facile de proposer une estimation sur son rendement et, donc, le bailleur était en droit d'exiger de son locataire tant de *gur* d'orge par *iku*.

2.5. Selon le „code" de Hammourabi, § 49, si un emprunteur qui donne un terrain à cultiver à son créancier, lui dit *esip tabal* „récolte (et) emporte", il l'autorise à se rembourser sur le revenu du champ. Les deux verbes à l'impératif constituent un syntagme qui fonctionne comme un élément de phrase (un monème lexical) au point de dépendre d'une préposition: il a loué *ana esip tabal* ou: ils ont partagé *ana esip tabal*, c'est-à-dire sur la base de la clause „récolte (et) emporte"[15].

2.6. La phrase *a-ḫi-is-sa e-ḫa-as-si, e-zé-eb-ša i-zé-eb-ši* (mot à mot: celui qui la prend, la prend; celui qui la laisse, la laisse)[16] ne prend son sens qu'en

---

12 Diverses variantes: *ina ālim, ana kima* uru.ki, ou à Emar, Emar, op. cit., nº 203,4': *ki-ma* uru-*li i-zu-zu*.

13 D. O. Edzard, *Altbabylonische Rechts- und Wirtschaftsurkunden aus Tell ed-Der*, 12; 20; 24; au nº 28: *ezib pî tuppi-šu*. Autre variante: *ana pî tuppi-šu labirim*, De Kiere, op. cit., 407.

14 YOS 12, nº 328. Au nº 146: *ki-ma i-mi-it-ti ù su-me-li* šà-ga al-du$_{10}$-ga.

15 CAD E, p. 330b, s.v. *esēpu*. L'expression a un emploi limité à l'époque paléo-babylonienne et semble être tombée en désuétude après.

16 BIN 7, 173, 14-15.

situation, autrement dit, elle n'est intelligible que dans un contexte déterminé, en l'occurrence, dans le cas du mariage que contracte un homme avec deux soeurs: puisqu'il a épousé la première, il s'engage à épouser la seconde, il est tenu dès lors, s'il répudie l'une des deux, de se séparer de l'autre. C'est une façon de préciser que le sort des deux femmes est lié. L'emploi du pluriel, variante qui est attestée, rendrait la clause plus explicite: *a-ḫi-zi-ma i-ḫa-zi-na-ti [e]-zi-ib-ši-na i-zi-ib-ši-na-ti*[17].

2.7. Le paiement, dans un acte de vente/achat, est évidement le point capital de la transaction et il arrive que l'une des parties éprouve des doutes. Ceux-ci sont levés par la mention *itti šalmi ù kini kasap-šu ilaqqe*, dont l'équivalent sumérien est ki lú.silim.ma.ta ù lú.gi.na.ta „il (= le vendeur) recevera son argent d'une personne en bonne santé (financière) et en qui on a confiance"[18]. En d'autres termes, le vendeur espère avoir affaire à quelqu'un de solvable qui, en outre, est bien la personne légalement responsable et, donc, tenue de remplir ses engagements.

2.8. On notera la tendance des lettrés accadiens à former des groupes de deux mots presque synonymes, ou du moins de sens voisin, sans que l'on puisse considérer, cependant, que l'un des deux soit inutile. Probablement, les clercs, avec leur esprit juridique déjà très chicanier, souhaitaient-ils prévoir toutes éventualités et ainsi prévenir les litiges.

Un exemple à Mari: *ina bītim u enūtim itallû* „ils seront privés de la maison et du mobilier"[19]. La redondance prévient la discussion qu'entamerait quelqu'un en prétendant que le terme *bītum* concerne uniquement la maison et non ce qu'elle contient.

De même, dans les baux relatifs à l'entretien des troupeaux, le berger se porte garant des animaux qui lui sont confiés: *ana pissâtim ù ḫalaqtim izzaz*. La phrase complète est: *ana pīḫāt pissâtim u ḫalaqtim izzaz*[20]. On insiste sur le fait que la perte d'un animal sera compensée, qu'il se soit égaré ou qu'il ait été volé, mais aussi qu'il soit mort d'une maladie (ici, peut-être, de la gale) ou de quelque épizootie. On envisage ainsi la disparition à l'intérieur de l'enclos comme à l'extérieur.

Les deux verbes *iḫalliq ittallakma* „s'il (= le travailleur loué) disparaît ou s'en va" sont quasi synonymes[21]. Ils sont juxtapposés et la particule *-ma* est

---

[17] TIM IV, 49.

[18] E. Szlechter, TJDB (Genève), p. 24; cf. CAD Š/1, s.v. *šalmu*, p. 260a.

[19] ARM VIII, 1, 10-11; cf. CAD E, 125a: 3 b 2'.

[20] E. Szlechter, TJDB, section V, Bail à cheptel, p. 104, pense à une perte „à l'intérieur" de l'enclos par l'opposition à *ḫaliqtum*, perte „à l'extérieur". AHw, p. 857a, s.v. *pessûm* „paralysie". Le CAD B, p. 156b „gale", trad. adoptée par A. Finet, *Code de Hammourabi*, p. 128, § 267.

[21] VAB V, n° 162.

placée à la fin du groupe, ce qui renforce l'unité de l'expression. Peut-être note-t-on une nuance un peu subtile? L'absence du travailleur est envisagée pour des motifs légèrement différents: il s'est enfui ou n'est pas venu pour une cause quelconque (parce qu'il était malade, par ex.). La série Ai, 7, IV, 15-19, a enregistré les cas où il n'aurait pas accompli les services exigés de lui; le clerc a procédé par accumulation: ba-ug$_x$, ba-an-záh, ugu-bi-an-dé-e, gàn la-ba-an-dag ù tu-ra ba-ab-AK = *imtūt, iḫtaliq, ittābata, ittaparka u imtaraṣu.* Si la mort (*imtūt*) et la maladie (*imtaraṣu*) sont des causes bien spécifiées, les autres éventualités, sans que les verbes soient des synonymes, ne sont guère différentes: il a disparu, il s'est enfui, il a cessé de travailler. Ce style s'explique par une volonté de n'omettre aucune cause d'absence, mais on peut supposer chez les juristes babyloniens une incapacité à l'abstraction.

Un locataire s'engage dans un bail *ana epēšim u wašābim.* On comprendra qu'il loue la maison avec l'intention de l'aménager et, ensuite, de l'habiter[22]. Un passage cité par CAD (A/2, p. 402b:c) indique clairement l'opération, car il y est fait allusion à un terrain „vide" (kislah) sur lequel le preneur construira une maison et l'habitera pendant dix ans.

3. Plusieurs des expressions figées que nous étudions ici, sont en réalité des métaphores; le contexte impose au lecteur de ne pas s'en tenir au sens litéral. Celui-ci, tiré du sens premier des mots, est tout à fait compréhensible, mais il ne veut rien dire dans un acte juridique.

3.1. Ainsi en est-il de la formule *eqlam mala maṣû* par laquelle les „notaires" indiquent la surface du champ loué: „field as far as it extends", selon la traduction proposée par le CAD (M/1, p. 345b) qui est, du reste, correcte. Toutefois, le verbe *maṣû* ne signifie pas „s'étendre", mais „être égal". Il y a déformation du sens premier: il s'agit d'un champ d'une superficie égale à ce qui est connu des deux parties et qui est situé là où chacun le sait[23]. La location ou la vente est un acte conclu *ex fide bona.* Le „notaire" ne donne pas la superficie exacte et se croit autorisé à épargner quelques lignes de texte.

3.2. La formule *mala maṣû* est remplacée par une autre, plus ou moins équivalente: *ma-la qa-as-su i-ka-aš-ša-du* „tout ce que sa main (celle du cultivateur) pourra atteindre"[24]. Elle est fondée sur une métaphore: la main est le symbole de la puissance de travail. Le champ est mis à la disposition du locataire qui en cultivera la part dont il est capable de s'occuper avec profit; de toute façon, il est stipulé qu'il remettra une quantité forfaitaire d'orge par *iku*

[22] E. Szlechter, TJDB, p. 64, 15.958,8.

[23] Dans les actes civils modernes, on trouve des phrases comme celle-ci: „terrain (ou maison, ou appartement) bien connu de l'acheteur".

[24] UET V, 212; cf. CAD K, p. 279b.

(36 ares). Cette pratique, comme cela se faisait en d'autres circonstances, suppose un mesurage au moment de la moisson.

3.3. On sait que, dans la plupart des langues, les métaphores dont l'élément essentiel est une partie du corps, sont très nombreuses. Le sumérien, et dans une plus large mesure l'accadien, n'échappent pas à cette règle. La main (sum. šu, acc. *qātum*) est la base de plusieurs verbes composés du type šu...teg/ti „approcher la main", donc „recevoir"[25]. En accadien, dans les contrats d'époque babylonienne ancienne, il est parfois prévu que le travailleur loué pour un mois „saisira la main pendant trois jours" (*ina* iti.1.kam u_4.3.kam *qātam iṣabbat*)[26]. Le sens de cette expression se déduit des faits: le travailleur fera trois jours supplémentaires pour le salaire d'un mois, ce qui impliquerait qu'il a bénéficié de trois jours de repos. Mais comment expliquer l'expression elle-même? Ou bien le sujet de *iṣabbat* est l'employeur: „saisir la main" signifierait alors „le retenir" au-delà du service; ou bien le sujet est l'ouvrier: „saisir la main" équivaudrait à „redevenir le maître de soi-même"[27], c'est-à-dire libre pendant quelques jours durant le mois, mais, si cette satisfaction est accordée, elle va de pair avec une compensation, d'où l'idée de trois jours supplémentaires.

3.4. Chaque fois, nous nous trouvons devant un problème particulier. Par exemple, avec *aḫam nadûm* „être négligent" dont on a de nombreuses attestations. Le verbe *nadûm* a le sens premier de „jeter" et, par extension, „laisser, abandonner" (parmi d'autres dont le CAD N/1, p. 68b, a établi la liste). L'idée de „négligence" demande que *nadûm* soit accompagné d'un complément: *aḫam*, d'où mot à mot: „laisser tomber le bras"; le bras représente la force physique et, par conséquent, le travail. Cela n'empêche pas le verbe *nadûm* d'être employé seul: *irub, inaddi-ma...* „il est entré (en service), s'il est négligent..." (il perdra son salaire)[28].

Il semble que le sumérien gú...šub, enregistré dans les listes lexicographiques, soit un calque de l'accadien, et non l'original. Au contraire d'une expression comme gaba...ri (ri a le sens de *nadûm*): „jeter la poitrine vers (+

---

[25] Voir l'excursus sur šu ba-ti, dans D. O. Edzard, op. cit., p. 29. A. Falkenstein, NSGU III, p. 165 et AnOr 28, p. 123-124. Voir aussi les composés avec igi „oeil": igi...bar, igi...du_8 etc.

[26] L. Waterman, BDHP, n° 17. Dans YOS 13, n° 20: *i-na* iti-1-kam 3 *u_4--mi qa-tam i-ṣa-bat*; dans YOS 12, n° 527: l'ouvrier devra neuf jours, car il a été loué trois mois. Formule parallèle: *i-na* iti 1 u_4-3-ka[m] *šu-zu-ub-tum* (YOS 12, 531. Cf. CAD Ṣ, p. 30a. L'interprétation est confirmée par le texte publié dans *De la Babylonie à la Syrie* (*Mélanges Kupper*), p. 41, n° 5: l'ouvrier est entré en service le 1er du 5e mois et le quittera le 30 du même mois, l'année suivante, donc un mois supplémentaire pour douze mois de travail.

[27] Comparer avec une des dernières lignes de l'inscription d'Utu-hegal (F. Thureau-Dangin, RA 9, p. 111, tranche): nam-lugal Ke-en-gi-ra šu-ba im-mi-gi_4 „il fit retourner la royauté de Sumer dans sa main", ce qui signifie que Sumer est redevenu indépendant.

[28] YOS 14, n° 48: *i-na-di-ma*; n° 7: *i-na-ad-di-ma*.

Loc.-Term.)", d'où: se présenter devant quelqu'un", comme dans l'exemple suivant: lugal.e gaba i.íb.re.eš „ils se présentèrent devant le roi"[29]. Le sumérien est plus imagé que l'accadien *maḫārum* qui lui correspond.

Le passage suivant montre une redondance *imḫur pāni-šu iškun* „il se présenta et parut" (devant les juges)[30]. Dans *pāni-šu iškun*, il est facile de reconnaître le sumérien igi...gar, qui figure à plusieurs reprises dans les minutes de procès et signifie simplement „il s'est présenté" pour expliquer ceci ou cela, pour accuser ou se justifier[31]. On pouvait aussi s'engager à ne pas „se présenter", c'est-à-dire à ne pas entamer une procédure de réclamation: u$_4$.kúr.šè NP igi.ni nu.gá.gá.àm[32]. En revanche, en accadien, y a-t-il pléonasme? Pour l'éviter, le CAD Š/1, p. 140, propose la traduction „se tourner vers quelqu'un avec confiance", l'accadien aurait ainsi ajouté une connotation qui n'affecte pas le sumérien. Mais est-elle justifiée?

3.5. L'idée de totalité est rendue par *ištu pî adi ḫurāṣim*[33], „depuis la balle de grain jusqu'à l'or" c'est-à-dire l'opposition entre les deux extrêmes: la balle du grain (*pûm* II, AHw, p. 874b, différent de *pûm* I „la bouche"), qui représente, parmi les objets, ce qui a le moins de valeur, et l'or, ce qu'il y a de plus précieux. Tout ce qui s'échelonne entre l'un et l'autre est évidemment compris.

4. En général, les relations juridiques comportaient, surtout dans les temps anciens, divers gestes et actes bien définis, accomplis au moment où le contrat était conclu. L'accord était ainsi solennisé devant témoins par une symbolique. E. Cassin a bien montré que l'empreinte du pied sur un terrain marque la prise de possession[34]. Dans les documents sumériens du IIIe millénaire, relatifs à l'achat d'une maison, on lit à la fin cette curieuse constatation: „son clou a été planté dans le mur"[35].

---

[29] BE 6, n° 10. Cf. A. Falkenstein, NSGU I, p. 60, note 9.

[30] PBS 5, 100, 2-3, cité par A. Falkenstein, ibid., qui critique les traducteurs qui cherchent à éviter le pléonasme.

[31] A. Falkenstein, op. cit., I, p. 122.

[32] UET V, n° 190, rev. 2. Il est stipulé „qu'à l'avenir, NP ne se présentera pas", sous-entendu: pour entamer une procédure de réclamation (gá.gá, forme *ḫamtu* de gar).

[33] E. Szlechter, TJDB, p. 12, 15.913, 28.

[34] E. Cassin, *Symboles de cession immobilière dans l'ancien droit mésopotamien*, republié dans *Le semblable et le différent, Symbolisme du pouvoir dans le Proche-Orient ancien* (Paris 1987) p. 280-337; voir en particulier p. 294. On y ajoutera Emar VI/3, n° 217: la vente par leurs parents de quatre enfants et, aux n° 218, 219 et 220, les empreintes de pied de trois d'entre eux; ces empreintes elles-mêmes furent authentifiées par les sceaux de deux témoins chaque fois.

[35] M. Malul, OA 26, p. 17; kak-bi é-gar$_8$-ra bí-rú, D. O. Edzard, op. cit., n° 31, 32... D'autres gestes: se frapper le front: *pussu imḫaṣ* signifie „se porter garant"; raser le coupable: *ugallabu* (Ai. 2, IV; 7,III,26-27); casser le pot: *kar-ba-sà ḫa-pi-at, qa-ab-li-it-sà še-eb-re-et* (CT 48,49, voir M. Vanderdriessche, Akkadica 42 (1985) p. 25-31. À Emar, à l'achat d'une maison, du pain est émietté et la table est ointe:

Le problème que nous voudrions essayer de résoudre maintenant est d'un autre ordre. L'expression figée mentionne bien un geste réel, comme ceux qui viennent d'être cités, mais elle ne vise pas à confirmer ou à solenniser les dispositions du contrat, elle les complète. Sa particularité est d'être un signe, doit-on même penser qu'il était exécuté? Ne serait-il alors qu'une simple allusion à un rite ancien que les gens de l'époque comprenaient mais que nous devons interpréter?

4.1. La symbolique du vêtement nous fournit un bon exemple. À Emar ou à Ugarit, plusieurs documents font allusion, à propos du non respect d'engagements familiaux, à l'obligation encourue par la personne qui a eu un comportement indigne, de „déposer son vêtement sur un tabouret et de s'en aller où cela lui plaît": túg-*šu ina* giš.šú.a *liškun, ašar* šà-*šu lillik*[36]. Cette clause prévoit que le coupable, rejeté par sa famille, la quittera en n'emportant rien de ce qui lui avait été donné en cadeau ou dont il bénéficiait en vertu d'un contrat de mariage ou d'adoption. Il semble inutile, dans la traduction, d'ajouter *naked* comme le fait le CAD. E. Cassin pense cependant que, dans certains cas, on arrachait le vêtement de l'épouse ou de la veuve coupable et qu'on la chassait nue, voire même qu'on l'exposait dans cet état *coram populo* pour l'humilier[37]. Le vêtement abandonné, à Emar, me semble plutôt être une synecdoque, il représente l'ensemble des biens qu'on n'a pas le droit de conserver. On comparera avec ce passage de la loi des XII Tables, à Rome, rapporté par Cicéron (*Phil.* 2,28,69) et qui présente une forme adoucie et plus policée de se comporter: *illam suam suas res sibi habēre jussit ex XII Tabulis claves ademit, exegit*: „il (Marc Antoine) ordonna à cette fameuse femme d'emporter avec elle ses frusques, selon (la loi) des XII Tables, il reprit les clés, il la mit à la porte". La concubine d'Antoine conserve ses propres biens, mais non ceux dont elle disposait. À Nuzi aussi, l'ourlet et la frange du vêtement jouaient un rôle, comme l'atteste l'expression *qannam ṣabātu/nakāsu*; couper la frange de la robe et laisser partir sa propriétaire paraît une sanction atténuée. Il est parfois difficile de décider si le geste, juridiquement prévu, était exécuté ou si, comme le constate Malul[38] il s'agit d'une „legal figure of speech rather than a symbolic act".

Le vêtement est ce que tout individu a de plus proche; c'était dans les temps anciens, souvent une caractéristique de sa personnalité, de son statut

---

ninda *ḫu-ku ka-si*$_{17}$*-ip* (giš)banšur ì-giš *pa-ši-iš* (Emar VI/3, n° 20; 130, 16-17). M. Malul a consacré un ouvrage à ces questions: *Studies in Mesopotamian Legal Symbolism* (= AOAT 221), Neukirchen 1988.

[36] Emar, op. cit., 5,30,32; cf. CAD S, p. 223b : 3'.

[37] E. Cassin, *Pouvoirs de la femme et structures familiales*, RA 63 (1969) p. 121-148; voir les p. 136 et suiv.

[38] M. Malul, op. cit., p. 239.

social. S'en dépouiller, c'est changer ses particularités[39]. Ainsi dans les décisions judiciaires, sous la 3e dyn. d'Ur, on lit: NP (qui a été affranchie) túg in.ùr „elle a lacéré son vêtement", elle est donc devenue une autre. À plusieurs reprises, le complément de la forme verbale est affecté du suffixe -ta, marquant la séparation, l'éloignement, d'où l'idée de „renoncer": à épouser tel jeune homme, à sa qualité d'épouse[40].

Ne quittons pas la symbolique du vêtement sans signaler cette phrase dans un contrat de mariage: NP(f) NP2(m) nam.dam.šè in.tuk... giš.igi.dù nu.mu.un.zu.na in.du$_8$ „NP2 a pris pour épouse NP, il a ouvert la fibule de (son épouse) vierge". Il s'agit de la fibule qui retient le vêtement féminin; si le mari l'a détachée, on laisse entendre que le mariage a été consommé[41]. Cette façon de s'exprimer est un euphémisme qu'éclaire le passage d'une tablette relative à l'*ardat lili*: ki.sikil lú.guruš.sa$_6$.ga giš.igi.dù nu.ba.ab.du$_8$.a = MIN (*ardatu*) *ša et-lu dam-qu ṣil-la-ša la-a ip-ṭu-ru* „la jeune fille dont un beau jeune homme n'a pas détaché la fibule"; la série des causes qui expliquent l'attitude méchante de l'*ardat lili* relèvant de la frustration sexuelle, il est facile de déterminer l'interprétation[42].

4.2. Les *nadītu*, riches et très avisées, et qui étaient de redoutables femmes d'affaires, exigeaient de leurs fermiers qu'ils déposent l'orge de la redevance *ina bab* gá.gi.a „à la porte du béguinage", ce qui se comprend: elles n'avaient pas les moyens de faire le transport elles-mêmes. En revanche, que signifie une livraison d'orge *ina pî aptim*? La traduction littérale „devant l'ouverture de la fenêtre" est manifestement insuffisante[43].

Dans bien des cas, la *nadītum* règle un achat *ina šawiriša* „avec son bracelet"[44]. La forme du mot offre plusieurs variantes ou un curieux mélange de

---

[39] Comme l'a bien vu E. Cassin, art. cité, p. 138-139. La comparaison avec Ištar dépouillée de ses vêtements quand elle entre dans les Enfers ne me semble pas pertinente, les circonstances sont tout à fait différentes.

[40] A. Falkenstein, NSGU II, n° 78; comment. en I, p. 76, note 3. Le suffixe -ta: n° 184, 2-5; 207, 15-16; suffixe -ra: n° 178, 20-21.

[41] TIM 4, 48 (daté de Rim-Sîn 2). Le terme sumérien giš-igi-dù (lecture dala) = accadien *ṣillû* (CAD Ṣ, p. 193). Sur l'interprétation de ce document, cf. R. Westbrook, *Old Babylonian Marriage Law* (AfO Beih. 23, 1988) p. 52 et la note 26; traduction p. 132. La fibule pourrait aussi être un euphémisme pour l'hymen, d'où „détacher l'hymen = déflorer la jeune fille".

[42] S. Lachenbacher, *Note sur l'*ardat lilî, RA 65 (1971) p. 136, 22'-24'.

[43] L'expression apparaît fréquemment, avec variantes, dans De Kiere, n° 188: *ina pî aptim ina* (giš) *mešiqum* (sic!); n° 204: *ina* ká *gagîm ina* ka *aptim*; n° 208: *ina mešeqi ina pî apti*; n° 175, 244, 249, 253... Le passage de Ai. 3, I, 21-23, ne fournit pas d'éclaircissement.

Un document publié dans *Annual Review of the RIM Project* 7 (1989) p. 41, 36 (daté de Samsu-iluna 6) a noté une curieuse mention: 20 *sila* d'orge pour l'achat de déportées (*ana nasḫatim*) *ana aptim ša gagîm* „à la fenêtre du béguinage". S'agit-il de déverser l'orge devant une fenêtre d'où l'on peut exercer un contrôle *de visu*?

[44] E. Szlechter, TJDB, p. 43, 16.516,4'; p. 45, 19.935,11. Cf. CAD S, s.v. *semeru*, p. 223b : 2a2'.

sumérien et accadien: *ina* ḫar kù.babbar-*ša*. La *nadītum* remettait au vendeur un bracelet d'argent d'un poids déterminé, comme prix du terrain ou de l'esclave. L'allusion aux bijoux de la dame pourrait être symbolique; selon l'interprétation de E. Szlechter, la mention du bracelet voudrait dire: la *nadītum* a payé avec son propre argent. On sait, en effet, que de nos jours encore, les femmes bédouines au Proche-Orient sont couvertes de bijoux, particulièrement des bracelets, qui constituent leur avoir personnel.

4.3. On se demande quelle est la tâche confiée à un travailleur engagé *ana šipir erēbim ù waṣîm* „pour le travail d'entrer et de sortir"[45]. D'après les exemples recueillis par le CAD E p. 263a, l'association des deux verbes opposés a une connotation de liberté. Entrer et sortir, c'est aller où l'on veut, décider soi-même de se déplacer; ce serait ici „faire ou ne pas faire quelque chose". Dans une lettre de Mari[46], Ibri-Dagan se plaint de ce que les hommes d'une tribu „vont et viennent" (*irubu uṣṣû*) auprès de leurs femmes résidant en dehors de la ville et, en réalité, ont la possibilité de fournir des renseignements à l'ennemi; aller et venir (l'accadien n'emploie pas la conjonction de coordination) est à prendre ici au premier degré, mais, comme nous l'avons déjà remarqué, il est possible que, dans un contexte juridique, l'expression soit métaphorique: la personne engagée travaillera sans surveillance ou seulement quand on aura besoin de ses services.

4.4. Au point de vue de la sémantique, la difficulté vient, dans certaines expressions, de ce que, en accadien, un verbe y a un complément qui ne paraît pas compatible[47]. C'est le cas du verbe *rašûm* „obtenir", qui a déjà été examiné ailleurs. F. R. Kraus[48] a montré que *pānam išum* „avoir une face, un devant" signifiait „être clair, évident", le visage permet d'identifier quelqu'un. Par conséquent, „obtenir une face" a le sens de „réussir à être reconnu"; à la forme III, *pānam šuršûm*, veut dire „faire que l'on soit reconnu", d'où la traduction de *awatam pānam lušarši* par „qu'il rende l'affaire claire". Quant au groupe *ḫititam rašûm*, il a été expliqué par A. Finet[49]; à la forme I/2, la traduction s'impose: „il prend la faute sur lui", d'où „il est responsable".

---

45 VAB V, n° 163.

46 ARM III, 16,15.

47 H. Weinrich, *Grammaire textuelle du français* (nous citons la trad. franç., Paris 1989) p. 271-2. Dans le syntagme „le triangle équilatéral", la présence de l'adjectif impose de considérer le triangle comme une forme géométrique; au contraire, dans le syntagme „triangle érotique", l'adjectif enlève au mot triangle son sens premier et l'on est obligé de comprendre qu'il s'agit du trio „mari, femme, maîtresse" ou „femme, mari, amant". Ce serait, pour Weinrich, la base de toute métaphore.

48 F. R. Kraus, *Akkadische Wörter und Ausdrücke* II, RA 64 (1970) p. 55-59.

49 A. Finet, ibid., p.172, à propos du § 267 du Code de Hammourabi.

Curieusement, on lit, dans une lettre de Mari, l'expression sans doute familière: *pānam u bābam ul išû* „ils n'ont ni devant ni porte"[50], sont ainsi désignés des gens dont on ne sait pas grand chose et qu'on ne dénombre même pas.

4.5. Ajoutons cette synecdoque qu'on lit dans un contrat de travail: *mimman ina qāti-šu innammar-ma ina idi-šu itelli* „si on trouve quelque chose dans sa main, il perdra son salaire"[51]. Un des rares moyens que l'on ait de prouver que le serviteur indélicat a volé, est qu'on le surprenne tenant en main l'objet dérobé, autrement dit: il faut le prendre en flagrant délit ou s'enfuyant avec l'objet en main. Le cas est bien connu en droit romain: *fur manifestus* (étymologie possible: le voleur „tenant la chose en main"). Si le voleur n'est pas pris sur le fait, il est difficile de le confondre, comme le montre le § 9 du Code de Hammourabi qui envisage les échappatoires avancées par le prétendu coupable[52].

5. Les expressions figées font partie du répertoire des „notaires". Ce sont, soit des formules qui constituent des habitudes de style, soit des métaphores traditionnelles, soit des groupes de mots qui doivent être considérés, parfois, comme des unités nominalisées. Nous avons fait remarquer plus haut que *esip tabal* formait un groupe qui dépendait de la préposition *ana*. Une autre preuve est fournie par ce passage: *tuppa-šu* NP *ina šeweri-ša išâm ul ša-*[*ṭir*] „il n'est pas écrit sur sa (masc.) tablette «elle a acheté avec son anneau»„[53]. Ce langage des clercs forme un ensemble de „signes" qui ne peuvent être compris que par référence à une culture juridique bien établie.

[50] ARM II, 99,10; Ch.-F. Jean a traduit „(ils) ne possèdent aucun recours". La traduction proposé par le CAD B, p. 25:f5b, rend mieux l'étonnement de l'expéditeur (Asqudum) qui se trouve en présence d'une masse de serviteurs, d'esclaves et d'animaux à propos desquels il ne sait rien.

[51] A. P. Riftin, SVJAD, nº 38.

[52] Sur les difficultés de la preuve, même dans la flagrance, voir les p. 198-9 de mon article *La maîtrise du temps en droit mésopotamien ancien*, dans *Cinquante deux réflexions sur le Proche-Orient ancien* (Mél. De Meyer, Leuven 1994).

[53] CT 52, 19, 20, cité par CAD S, p. 223.

OLD ARAMAIC CONTRACTS OF GUARANTEE

Edward Lipiński

The bilingual Assyro-Aramaic archive from the Gōzān – Ḫarrān area, in the collections of the Royal Museum of Art and History in Brussels,[1] contains a few contracts of guarantee, written on clay tablets in the Aramaic semi-cursive script of the 7th century B.C. In law, as well known, a guarantee is a contract to answer for the payment of some debt, or the performance of some duty, in the event of the failure of another person who is primarily liable for such payment or performance. In order that there may be a contract of guarantee there is no need of a distinct document signed or legalized by the parties, but there must be a primary liability, present or future, of a principal debtor, and a promise made for a valuable consideration by a third party to the creditor to discharge that liability if the principal debtor does not. This third party is called the «surety» or «guarantor». His promise must be such that liability only arises in the event of the failure of the principal debtor to meet his obligations. Ancient Oriental law does not seem to distinguish a contract of guarantee from a contract of indemnity which establishes an original liability to indemnify the creditor against any loss which he may incur in letting a third party have some specified goods.

A sketch of ancient West Semitic guarantee[2] is to be found in the biblical Book of Proverbs, where the surety's undertaking is described as given verbally and accompanied not by a handshake but by a strike of the creditor's hand in order to show agreement and to signify the assumption of an obligation[3]:

«My son, if you have stood surety for your fellow,

---

[1] These texts will be published in D. Homès-Fredericq - P. Garelli - E. Lipiński, *Archives d'un centre provincial de l'Empire assyrien* (*Documents du Proche-Orient ancien. Epigraphie 2*), forthcoming. Several preliminary studies have appeared in various journals and proceedings; most of them are quoted by E. Lipiński, *Aramaic Clay Tablets from the Gozan-Harran Area*, JEOL 33 (1993-94), p. 143-150 (see p. 143, n. 1).

[2] The topic is discussed by E. Lipiński, *Gage et cautionnement chez les Sémites du Nord-Ouest*, in J. Zabłocka - S. Zawadzki (eds.), *Šulmu IV. Everyday Life in Ancient Near East* (Poznań 1993) p. 213-222, with former literature, but without a detailed discussion of the Aramaic tablets.

[3] Prov. 6, 1-5; see also Prov. 11, 15; 17, 18; 22, 26.

have struck your hand for a stranger,
have been caught by the words of your mouth,
trapped yourself by the words of your mouth,
do now this, my son, and free yourself,
for you are come in your fellow's power:
Go, bestir yourself, and pester your fellow,
give not sleep to your eyes
nor slumber to your eyelids.
Free yourself like a gazelle from his power,
like a bird from the hand of the fowler».

The Hebrew phrase signifying that someone stands surety is *tāqa' kāp*[4] or *tāqa' lə-yād* (Job 17,3), while its Old Aramaic equivalent is *mḥ' yd*,[5] attested also in contemporary Neo-Assyrian deeds under the form *qātāti maḫāṣu*.[6] An unpublished Aramaic deed in private hands, dating back also to the 7th century B.C., uses the phrase *mḥ' b-yd* (line 12), exactly like Dan. 4,32, but it does not belong to the bilingual archive kept in Brussels. The suretyship bears there on the payment of a sum of 20 shekels of silver by a certain Mati'-Ši', *ksp* 20 *šqln mt'š' yšlm.*

The Aramaic expression *mḥ' yd* occurs in a loan contract from the time of Ḫarrānay,[7] the second incumbent of the archive from the Gōzān – Ḫarrān area. The text is inscribed on a triangular docket and seems to be the summary of a contract: the full text was most likely written on a piece of parchment or leather, rolled and sealed with the help of the docket.[8]

š'rn 3 zph	«Barley, 3 (ḥomers), loan
zy hrn 'l	of Ḫarrān(ay)[9] for
bty w'l ḥgny	Batay and for Ḥaggānay.[10]
bršmš	Bar-Šamaš
mḥ' yd	struck the hand».

[4] Prov. 6, 1; 17, 18; 22, 26; Nah. 3, 19; see also Prov. 11, 15.
[5] *Maḥa' bə-yad* occurs in Dan. 4, 32.
[6] K. Deller, in Or 53 (1984), p. 76; *CTN* III, p.58. Mrs K. Radner deals with that subject in her work *Die neuassyrischen Privatrechtsurkunden als Quelle für Mensch und Umwelt* (Helsinki 1997) p. 362-367.
[7] O.3658, to be published by E. Lipiński in op.cit. (n. 1), No. 50.
[8] See J. N. Postgate, *Fifty Neo-Assyrian Documents* (Warminster 1976) p. 5-6, § 1.2.3.
[9] The name of the creditor is written here without final *y*, as in No. 54,4 of the same archive. On this name, cf. E. Lipiński, *The Personal Names Handî, Harrānay, and Kurillay in Neo-Assyrian Sources*, in H. Hauptmann - H. Waetzholdt (eds.), *Assyrien in Wandel der Zeit* (Heidelberger Studien zum Alten Orient 6 (Heidelberg 1997) p. 89-93.
[10] Tentative vocalization, based on Syriac *ḥaggānāyā*, «festal».

The names of the four witnesses, written on the reverse, are illegible, but the date - probably *yrḥ* [*s*]⌜*mn*⌝ *h*, «eighth month»[11] – and the numeral *2* referring most likely to the two borrowers can still be read at the bottom of the docket.

Since the rate of interest is not mentioned, the amount of barley allegedly lent may include the interest,[12] probably 50%. The quantity of barley really lent would then amount to only two ḥomers or about 300 litres.[13] This barley was most likely needed to sow some 3,5 ha of farmland,[14] since the eighth month of the Assyrian calendar corresponds to October/November, which was the normal planting season, before the winter rains. Borrowings made during that period aimed mainly at acquiring seed suitable for sowing.

The borrowers are otherwise unknown, unless Batay is the lady ᶠ*Ba-ta-ia-a* mentioned in a somewhat older deed of the same archive.[15] In this case, Ḥaggānay might be her son. Despite the small amount of barley lent, and perhaps because the borrower was a lady, a certain Bar-Šamaš had to stand surety for them. The top of the tablet bears two impressions of shells used as seals.[16]

The phrase *mḥ' yd* occurs also in an earlier deed that dates from the time of Ḥaddiy,[17] the first incumbent of the archive, who was the steward of the local palace of the Queen Mother *Naqi'a-Zakûtu* and was active down to 665 B.C. The text does not specify the identity of the creditor that should be identified with the palace itself, the steward of which was Ḥaddiy who acts as surety in this circumstance.

š'rn. 'l. rp'n	«Barley for Rapa'ān
wšyr 10 *b* 10+3+2	and Šāyir : 10 into 10+3+2.
wḥdy mḥ' yd	And Ḥaddiy struck the hand.
š'ry' hšhl	He delivered the barley.

[11] *Smnh* occurs in the same archive under No. 56, 8-9 (see also No. 45,4). It is a transcription of Neo-Assyrian *šamāne* or *šamānat*, «eight», and *yrḥ smnh* corresponds to Babylonian *Araḫsamna* and to later Aramaic *Marḥešwān*, «October/November».

[12] For this kind of loan contracts, that include the interest in the sum or amount of goods allegedly borrowed, see E. Lipiński, Nešek *and* tarbīt *in the Light of Epigraphic Evidence*, OLP 10 (1979), p. 133-141.

[13] A ḥomer or *imāru* is a donkey load, needed to sow 1 *imāru* of land. The available evidence is as yet insufficient to establish its absolute value in Assyria, as shown by M. A. Powell, *On the Absolute Value of the Assyrian* qa *and* emār, in Iraq 46 (1984), p. 57-61; cf. also id., in RLA VII, p. 487-488 and 500-502. Nowadays, an Iraqi donkey carries about 150 l of barley.

[14] M. A. Powell, in RLA VII, p. 487-488, considers that 1 *imāru* (ḥomer) corresponded to a surface of 1,8 ha.

[15] P. Garelli in op. cit. (n. 1), No. 2, 3.

[16] D. Homès-Fredericq, Glyptique sur les tablettes araméennes des Musées Royaux d'Art et d'Histoire, in RA 70 (1976), p. 57-70 (see p. 69).

[17] O.3670, to be published by E. Lipiński in op. cit. (n. 1), No. 47.

šhd[*n ḥ*]*lrm*	Witness[es : (A)ḥa]larīm
wnny	and Nanî.
wḥṣdn 7	And 7 reapers».

The amount of barley lent and the interest rate are specified in the present deed by means of the formula «10 (ḥomers increase) into 15 (ḥomers)», thus 50%. Ḥaddiy acts personally as guarantor and the text states that the barley has been delivered. This is expressed by the causative haf'el form of the verb *šhl* that corresponds to Assyro-Babylonian *šiālu*, «to pour out», and to Arabic *sahhala*, «to supply», «to provide». The names of the two witnesses are followed by the additional clause «and 7 reapers». This means that the loan includes a provision for the debtors to supply the creditor with seven reapers at harvest time. The exact meaning of this «harvester clause» appears from other contracts which enact, for instance, that the borrower «shall provide harvesters at the harvesting of the field; if they do not come, he shall give one mina of silver».[18] Such clauses may be considered as a form of additional interest charged on loans of grain. In this particular case, it may be justified by the guarantee offered by Ḥaddiy, thus entitled to a benefit arising in the guarantor's favour. Since Ḥaddiy possessed a stamp seal of his own, with his name engraved on the seal,[19] the nail impressions on the top of the tablet[20] must be considered as authentification signs apposed by the principal debtor, not by the guarantor.

The phrase *mḥ' yd* can be restored confidently in another conveyance from the time of Ḥaddiy.[21] The loan bears on four donkeys belonging to Ḥaddiy and lent to a certain Lā-qēpu. The name of the guarantor is lost, but there are two witnesses and a seal impression, stamped either by the principal debtor or by the guarantor.

ḥmr. lḥdy	«Donkey(s) belonging to Ḥaddiy
'l lqp 3+1	for Lā-qēpu : 3+1
[ ]	[P.N.]
[*mḥ'*]	[struck]

[18] BM 134554, lines 6-8, published by J. N. Postgate, *More 'Assyrian Deeds and Documents'*, Iraq 32 (1970) p. 129-164 and Pl. XVIII-XXXI (see p. 148-149 and Pl. XXV). A similar clause is found in the Aramaic deeds VA 7499, line 2, from Assur, K 3785, line 5, and BM 81-2-4, 147, line 5, both from Nineveh; cf. F. M. Fales, *Aramaic Epigraphs on Clay Tablets of the Neo-Assyrian Period* (Studi semitici NS 2, Roma 1986) Nos. 3, 9, and 47. This practice has a long history in Mesopotamia. The Neo-Assyrian evidence is discussed by J. G. Lautner, *Altbabylonische Personenmiete und Erntearbeiterverträge* (SDIO 1, Leiden 1936) p. 26-28, and by J. N. Postgate, op. cit. (n. 8), p. 44-45, § 3.5.

[19] It is impressed on the tablet O.3686, which will be published as No. 36.

[20] D. Homès-Fredericq, art. cit. (n. 16), p. 68-69.

[21] O.3646, to be published by E. Lipiński in op. cit. (n. 1), No. 46.

yd. šhd	the hand. Witness(es) :
hd'š	Had'āš
wddnwry	and Dadnûrî».

The concision of the text, that lacks any provisions for the borrower, can be explained only by the fact that the triangular docket is the summary of a full contract of guarantee, written on papyrus or on parchment.

The general requisites of a contract of guarantee in no way differ from those essential to the formation of any other contract, but West Semitic wisdom sentences, roughly contemporary with the Aramaic deeds, strongly exhort against undertaking a suretyship obligation because, if it is unfulfilled, the creditor might levy payment even on the surety's garments and bedding. This unfavourable attitude towards contracts of guarantee is expressed in ancient sections of the Hebrew Book of Proverbs[22] and it is reflected also, although to a lesser degree, in the work of Ben Sira[23] that dates from the second century B.C. Even in Talmudic times, i.e. in the Late Roman and Sassanid periods, suretyship is mentioned as one of the things a man is advised to avoid.[24]

The consequences possibly resulting from a contract of guarantee explain this negative attitude of the sages towards this particular form of agreements. The specific Old Aramaean requisites of a contract of guarantee are unknown, but the ancient Jewish practice is at least partly based on the same or on a similar jurisprudence.

At first Jewish law, as formulated in the Mishna, recognized suretyship only insofar as it was undertaken before or at the time of the principal debtor's liability, for in such a case the creditor «had lent him the money through his trust in the guarantor».[25] In the first half of the second century A.D., however, Rabbi Ishmael stated that a written contract of guarantee was valid even if it was signed or sealed after the creation of the principal obligation.[26] Some sages held that such a guarantee was valid even if it was given verbally, but the law practice rather followed the opinion of Simeon Ben Nanos, Ishmael's contemporary, who did not admit the validity of a guarantee given after the creation of the principal debtor's obligation, «since not through trust in him had the creditor lent the debtor money».[27] However, from the 4th century A.D. on, the opinion of Rabbi Nahman ben Jacob (d. c. 320 A.D.), a leading Babylonian sage of his time, found general acceptance to the effect that even a ver-

[22] Prov. 20, 16; 22, 27; 27, 13, and cf. here above.
[23] Sir. 8, 13; 29, 17-20.
[24] Babylonian Talmud, *Yebamot* 109a.
[25] Mishna, *Baba Batra* 10,8.
[26] Ibid. and Babylonian Talmud, *Ketubot* 101b-102a.
[27] Mishna, *Baba Batra* 10,8.

bal guarantee given after the creation of the principal liability was considered as valid in certain circumstances.[28] Nothing proves that such a practice was followed also in earlier periods, since a written suretyship accompanies even very small loans, as 2 or 3 ḥomers of barley like in the first case contemplated by the Aramaic deed from the archive of Ḥarrānay.

The symbolic striking of the hand, signified in Aramaic by the phrase *mḥ' yd*, must belong to a longstanding practice of Semitic legal customs, reaching almost the early times of the third millennium B.C., which are the favourite period of Dr. Krystyna Szarzyńska's research. In fact, the same phrase *ma-ḫa-ṣí i-da* occurs at Ebla in the bilingual vocabulary of the royal archive.[29] Although this formula lacks any context and does not refer necessarily to a contract of guarantee, it must express agreement and mutual consent of the parties, which is essential to the formation of any contract.

[28] Babylonian Talmud, *Baba Batra* 176a-b. Cf. Sh. Albeck, *Acquisition*, in *Encyclopaedia Judaica* 2 (Jerusalem 1971) col. 216-221, especially col. 219-220 (7), and M. Elon, *Suretyship*, in *Encyclopaedia Judaica* 15 (Jerusalem 1971) col. 524-529, in particular col. 524-525.

[29] G. Pettinato, *Testi lessicali bilingui della Bibliotheca L. 2769* (MEE 4, Napoli 1982) p. 375, No. 0411.

SOME REMARKS ON JEWELLERY IN THE OLD ASSYRIAN TEXTS

Krystyna Łyczkowska

Holding a belief that our celebrated colleague, a lover of Oriental jewellery, shall find these remarks on Old Assyrian women's ornaments infrequently found in the texts from Kaneš interesting, I would like to present this short paper.

Jewellery played an important role in the life of the ancient peoples of Mesopotamia. It served as adornment for men, women, and children. It was also an important element of the garments of gods' cultic images. It was used in burials or as *kispu* offerings.[1] The studies on Mesopotamian ornaments are based on the following sources: pieces of jewellery recovered during excavations, their representations on reliefs and statues, and from cuneiform texts.

Jewellery was made from precious metals (silver, gold, but also copper or bronze), stones (precious and semi-precious), covered with granulation and filigree; the techniques of production being specific for respective periods. Units of personal jewellery recorded in Akkadian texts from various periods are, i.a., rings *(šawiru/semeru, annuqu, ḫuppu,* or, perhaps, *ṣerretu? unqu)* worn on hands, arms or ankles; earrings *(anṣabtu/inṣabtu, qudāštu)*, head ornaments in the form of a tiara or crown *(āgu, mammu/memu, i/erretu)*, necklaces of various kinds *(erimmatu, kišadu, ḫišum, tudittu)*, fibulae, brooches, pins, etc. The appearance of these ornaments may be reconstructed on the basis of sculptures, bas-reliefs, or paintings representing them, or actual finds discovered by the archaeologists *in situ*.[2] The most difficult problem is connected with the names: it is difficult to link the Akkadian name of the object with the actually existing or represented in a work of art ornament; it is not always possible to provide a univocal translation of the Akkadian names of respective ornaments. The Babylonians recorded the name of the object, often also the material from

---

[1] Cf. the list of funerary offerings buried with the dead from Old Babylonian Period, CT 45,99:6-9; Akio Tsukimoto, in: RAI XXI, p. 129; cf. Fs. Hrouda, 235.

[2] The most famous collection comes from the royal graves at Ur; 3 royal tombs from Nimrud contained the most magnifical jewellery from the first mill. B.C.

which it was made, sometimes its weight, but there are no precise descriptions of the appearance of the objects in question.

Mentions of ornaments *(šukuttum)* appear in literature (myths, epos, hymns, or prayers) and economic texts. However, there are no mentions of the techniques applied by the goldsmith *(kutimmu)*, methods of making and adorning respective pieces of jewellery, of the technology used by the artisans-goldsmiths. It should be, however, remembered that jewellery was a prize desired by all the invaders and the fact that it was transported to various areas makes it difficult to determine where it was produced. Jewellery was made most probably to order (it may believed that the royal court had a goldsmith), although in later periods there existed workshops which produced jewellery and sold it.

This short paper shall deal with the mentions of jewellery pieces appearing in some economic texts or letters coming from Kaneš, an Old Assyrian colony in Asia Minor, in the early 2nd millennium B.C.

Family letters, orders, or lists of goods sent from Kaneš to Aššur or from Aššur to Cappadocia, as well as receipts for consignments mention, i.a., pieces of jewellery as goods or ornaments for personal use. It should be stressed that in the large body of texts written by Old Assyrian merchnats, little definite information about the quality and types of ornaments can be found. Only in later texts (e.g., from the Old Babylonian period, texts from Mari and later ones) these mentions are more numerous.[3] Old Assyrian texts contain, most often, information that large quantities of gold or silver as well as precious stones[4] meant for trade were sent. In this paper we focus on the mentions of jewellery products made for private use. These products were to be used mainly by women: the merchants' wives and daughters, and were meant as proof of their social status and wealth. It can not be excluded, however, that they were sent to give the women pleasure.

It should be remarked that the data on the Old Assyrian ornaments is drawn mainly from texts of various contenents.[5]

The reflections presented below are based on the correspondence between Pūšukēn, the most prominent member of the Cappadocian colonies, and Lamassi, a married couple known from numerous documents from Kaneš. The

---

[3] Cf. ARM XXI, nr 247 ff.

[4] Cf. C. Michel, *Innaya dans les tablettes paléo-assyriennes* Vol. I, II (Paris 1991); M. T. Larsen, *The Old Assyrian City-State and its Colonies* (Copenhagen 1976) p. 199.

[5] Same archeological evidences: bracelets, pectorals, pins, finger rings, earrings from gold, silver or copper there are uncovered at Aššur and Kaneš in several graves, cf. K. R. Maxwell-Hyslop, *Western Asiatic Jewellery c. 3000-612 B.C.* (London 1971) 70 f, 97 ff; B. Musche, *Vorderasiatischer Schmuck von den Anfängen bis zur Zeit der Achaemeniden* (Leiden 1992) 141 ff. Taf. XLIX; J. G. Drecksen, *The Old Assyrian Copper Trade in Anatolia* (Istanbul 1996) p. 248 ff.

wife stayed in Aššur, and the male part of the family, in Kaneš, where they carried out large business. The Pūšukēn family was linked with other merchant families known from the preserved texts. The text No 42 published in VAS X (E. Klengel-Brandt and C. Veenhoff) served as a starting point because it mentions certain ornaments which Pūšukēn meant for his wife Lamassi and daughter Aḫaḫa/Waqurtum, a priestess. The letters between Pūšukēn and Lamassi reveal personal interest and care about the family manifested by both parents. Particular graces were bestowed upon the daughter-priestess, whose mother often wrote about her to Pūšukēn, and repeatedly reminded him of his duty to come to Aššur to perform the traditional rites connected with the ceremony of dedicating the daughter to god: „the girl has grown up, be so kind and come to lie her in Aššur's bosom."[6]

In the second part of the paper, in order to illustrate the range of names of ornaments, fragments of texts containing mentions of jewellery are presented.

Fragment of a letter from Lamassi to Pūšukēn (see also the list, No 9):

> [1]a-na Pu-šu-ki-in qí-bi-ma [2] um-ma La-ma-sí-ma... [14]a-pu-tum i-ḫi-id-ma [15]pu-[uḫ] a-ni-qí ša ṣu-ḫa-ri [16]ša ta-ap-tu-ru [17]KÙ.GI še-bi-lam-ma a-ni-qi [18]lá-áš-ku-šu-nu-ma li-ba-šu-nu [19]lá i-lá-mi-in KÙ.GI [20] ša Bu-za-zu ša te-zi-bu [21]ḫi-ti a-na A-ḫa-ḫa e-pu-uš [22]a-na mu-zi-zi-ká [23]lá ta-ša-la-at
>
> From Lamassi to Pūšukēn...: please watch out (be careful); in return for the ring (belonging) to the boy which you bought – send me gold so that I can give them rings to wear and they will not be angry. From the gold of Buzazu which you have left, make *ḫittu* for Aḫaḫa. Do not act high-handedly with your agents.

Two problems are discussed here: firstly, in return for the ring bought by Pūšukēn, which belonged to a boy (whose name is not mentioned) Lamassi demands gold to satisfy the creditors. Secondly, she asks Pūšukēn to have a ring made for Aḫaḫa, the daughter-priestess, probably for her own use. The second document (text No 13), a letter from Pūšukēn to Lamassi, in the part connected with the subject matter of this paper, contains a list of the goods and jewellery sent for sale or to hand over or return to other merchants, e.g., one mina of silver price for either a ring or a belt for a boy, its weight being 42 1/2 shekels and a ring; all that is brought to Lamassi by Dan-Aššur. Moreover, Pūšukēn obliges Lamassi to hand over to Dan-Aššur his bracelets or the belt for the boy. In another letter, from Pūšukēn (text No 20) addressed to Aššur-bani, Šalim-Aššur, and Ikunum, the sender informs about the consignment of the bracelet for the girl which is worth one mina of silver, a golden ring worth 18 shekels, and 2 *miḫṣu*, *ḫittu* and *tudinatu*. The *nisḫatu*-tax for these was added. It may be assumed that these objects were meant for Pūšukēn's daughter, Aḫaḫa.

---

[6] I.e., dedicate her to god, see K. Łyczkowska, in: Drevnij Vostok IV, 68[10].

Text No 32 which is an anonymous report, mentions Lamassi and Aḫaḫa as the recipients of two pectorals weighing 1/3 mina (probably of silver).

These mentions allow us to assume that women of Pūšukēn's family not only handed over and sold jewellery or precious stones as well as played the role of agents, but were themselves given them. It should be added that the main task of women living in Aššur (besides taking care of the home and family) was making cloth for sale in Anatolia; some of them also served as agents in purchasing various products or raw materials for their male relations in Cappadocia.[7]

Other women, merchants' wives from Kaneš, mentioned below, received similar consignments of silver, gold, ornaments, etc, e.g., Taram-Kubi, wife of Innaja, Tariš-matum, sister of Pūšukēn, wife of Aššur-malik, and others, belonging mainly to the first generation of Assyrian merchants in Kaneš. They received small amounts of silver or gold sent from Cappadocia to Aššur. It was quite natural that their husbands and male relatives living in Anatolia sent some valuables. The women needed financial means to run the household. They occasionally received presents: jewellery, ornaments, luxury goods, votive gifts; it was not rare in affluent societies. The lists of items sent from Anatolia contain even gifts exchanged by women in Cappadocia and Aššur. It should not be forgotten, however, that the Cappadocian documents mention merchants and not the higher social strata, which, thanks to their affluence and, probably, custom, posessed large numbers of ornaments, probably of greater value. Ornaments are mentioned quite rarely, which may have many reasons. I do not believe that it is because the sources do not represent the whole material. Earrings, so common in Mesopotamian ornaments mentioned in texts or appearing on bas-reliefs, appear in the texts from Kaneš here presented only once. *Annuqu* are mentioned 8 times, *ḫittu*, 3 times, *kišadu*, twice, *šawiru*, 9 times, and *tudittu*, as much as 13 times. The *tudittu* may have several meanings (see the remarks below). For a slightly later, Old Babylonian, period, from Mari, there are more diversified lists of objects; it should be stated, however, that these are ornaments of people most probably connected with the court.

As it has been said above, the amount of information about jewellery found in a considerable number of Cappadocian texts is surprisingly scant; there are no mentions of many ornaments known from Old Babylonian texts or later records. The list of personal ornaments quoted below comes from the documents found in the house of Pūšukēn and those of other known and affluent Old Assyrian merchants.

---

7 Lamassi was an agent for the unknown form of purchasing tin and cloth „from Agade".

annunqu – according to CAD A_{II},142a, (only OA) „a piece of jewellery" (there are no particular reasons to connect it with *unqu* – ring); according to AHw 52 b *annaqu* – „Ring – aA; statt sonst *unqu*". In this paper – ring.

1. ATHE 8:8 Memorandum

2/3 GÍN 15 ŠE [2]KÙ.BABBAR a-na [3]ug-ba-áb-tim [4]ša a-ni-qí [5] a-na Aḫ-Ištar [6]tù-kà-i-lu [7]áš-qúl

I have paid 2/3 of shekel and 15 ŠE of silver to the *ugbabtum* who held the ring of Aḫ-Ištar as pledge.

2. ATHE 39:29 Letter from Ili-wedakum to Puzur-Ašur

[28]10 GÍN KÙ.BABBAR [29]ší-im a-ni-qí-im [30]ša a-mu-tim ša Ḫu-ut-kà [31]ub-lá-ni ku-nu-ki-a [32] Ḫu-ut-kà na-áš-a-kum

Ḫutka has brought to me ten shekels of silver, the price of the ring of *amutum*[8] with my seal; Ḫutka is bringing it to you.

3. BIN VI 6:14 Letter from Ašur-rabi to Ab-šalim

[14]a-ni-qí ša KÙ.GI [15]šé-ṣí-e-im

Send me a gold ring.

4. CCT II 36a:20 Letter from Pūšukēn to Lamassi, see No 13 (sub:*šawiru*)

5. CCT III 24:4 *ibidem*, see No 14 (sub: *šawiru*)

6. KTK 68:1 Report

a-nu-qum ša a-mu-tim [2]ša a-na 15 GÍN KÙ.BABBAR [3]a-na ša-pár-tim i-ni-id-ú-ni

Ring of *amutum* which has been deposided as a pledge for 15 shekels of silver.

7. TCL IV 108:13 Transport contract

[13]2 a-né-qé-en <u> [14]ša-ḫi-re-en a-na [15]ṣú-ḫa-ri-im mì-ma a-ni-im [16] A-šùr-i-di [17] a- na A-lim^{KI} [18]ú-(šé)-bíl

Two rings (and) *šaḫiren (*anklets ?) [9] for a boy - all that Ašur-idi sent to City.

8. VAS X 42:14 ff Letter from Lamassi to Pūšukēn, see also No 13, 20, 32

[14]a-pu-tum i-ḫi-id-ma [15]pu-[ùḫ] a-ni-qí ša ṣú-ḫa-ri [16]ša ta-ap-ṭu-ru [17]KÙ.GI šé-bi-lam-ma a-ni-qí [18]lá-áš-ku-šu-nu-ma

Please watch out: (in return for) a ring (for) *ṣuḫaru*, which you bought, send gold so that I can give them rings to wear.

anṣabtu / inṣabtu – according to CAD A_{II} 144a „ring, earring"; AHw 54a – „Ring, Ohring". In this paper – earring, clip.

9. BIN VI 179, ff. Fragment of a letter (see also No 22)

---

8 *amutum* – (CAD A_{II} 97 b) – precious metal.

9 Or „and two rings with (matching) for the boy".

[5]ší-ta i-ṣa-áb-ta-an [6]ša NA_4.ZA.GÌN i-na lib-bi [7]ri-ik-si-im [8]ša-ak-na-ni-kum
Two earrings (decorated) with lapis lazuli are placed in the package for you.

ḫittu – CAD H 208b, „an object of precious metal"; AHw: no mention of aA. In this paper – ornament.

10. CCT III 29:26 Letter from *ša kima jâti* to Enlil-bani and Ašur-iddin; see No 25 (sub: *tudittu*)

11. TCL IV 30:13, Letter from Pūšukēn to Ašur-bani, Šalim-Ašur and Ikunum; see No 31 (sub: *tudittu*)

kišadu – CAD K 446,2 „necklace, piece of jewellery, etc."; AHw 490 sub: Schmuck. Not to be found in OA. In this paper – necklace.

12. ICK II 321: 11 Report
[11]20 ki-ša-dí ša zi-ga-ša-ri
Twenty necklaces with *zigašari*-beads(?).[10]

semeru/šawiru CAD S 219 i.a. „bracelet"; AHw 1036 „Ring als Schmuck". In this paper – bracelet.

13. CCT II 36a:17 Letter from Pūšukēn to Lamassi[11]
[17]lu ša-wi-ru lu mu-sà-ru-um[12] [18]ša ṣú-ḫa-ri-im [19]KI..LÁ.BI 2/3 MA.NA 2 1/2 GÍN [20]a-ḫa-ma a-nu-qù-šú ṣú-ḫa-<ra>-am [21]u [am]-tam mì-ma a-nim [22]Dan-A-šur i-ra-dí-a-ki-im [28]ša-wi-ri-šu ù mu-sà-ra-am [29]a-ṣe-er 1/3 MA.NA KÙ.BABBAR [30]ša a-di-nu-šu-nu a-na Dan- [A-šur] [31] dí-ni-ma
One third mina of silver (worth) either rings or a belt for a boy, its weight being 2/3 mina 1/2 shekel. Give (Lamassi) his rings and belts to Dan Ašur for 1/3 mina of silver.

14. CCT III 24:4,9 Letter from Taram-Kubi to Innaya. See C. Michel, vol. II, No 3
[4]ša-wi-ru-ú ù a-nu-qú-ú [5]ša i-ba-ší-ú-ni ša-ṣí-ri [6]a-na a-kà-li-ki li-ib-ši-ú [7]ke-na[!]-tim-ma 1/2 MA.NA KÙ.GI [8]Ili-ba-ni tù-šé-bi-lam [9]a-i-ú-tim [š]a-wi-ri [10]ša té-zi-ba-ni i-nu-mì [11]tù-úṣ-u KÙ.BABBAR 1 GÍN [12]ú-lá té-zi-ba-am
(You said): any bracelets and rings there are guard well, they should serve as your (Taram-Kubi) sustenance. Indeed, send me 1/2 mina of silver with Ili-Bani. 9-12 What silver bracelets did you leave me? When you departed, you did not leave me even one shekel of silver!

15. Hecker, Giessen 25:12 Memorandum
...[10] 1 MA.NA 17 GÍN KÙ.BABBAR[13] ša [11]GAL.ZABAR[14] [12]1 1/3 MA.NA KÙ.BABBAR ša-wi-ru?-ú [13]mì-ma a-nim a-na [14]Tariš-matum

---

[10] CAD K 448, but cf.the meaning of *zigašarru*, CAD Z 108a (a commodity); AHw – eine Ware.
[11] Cf. EL 112a.
[12] *miserru, musseru* CAD M_{II} 110b – belt, gridle.
[13] Cf. Veenhof, BiOr XXIV, 186 b.

1 mina 17 shekels (77 shekels) of silver, a bronze bowl, 1 1/3 MA.NA – (80 shekels) for the bracelet; all this (is transported) to Tariš-matum.

16. I 495 Transport contract[15]

[1]1 MA.NA KÙ.BABBAR ša-wi-ri [2]Ta-ra-am-Ku-bi [3]ù Ší-ma-at-A-šur [17]mì-ma a-nim šé-bu-lá-tim [18]ri-ik-sí ip-qí-dam

Ring of 1 mina of silver for Taram-Kubi and Simat-Ašur. This whole consignment of *riksu* he had entrusted to me.

17. Ka 1044 Letter from Imdi-ilu to Taram-kubi

[5]ša-wi-ri ša qá-tí-a [6]šu-qúl-ta-áš-nu 1 MA.NA KÙ.BABBAR [7]ku-nu-ki-a Puzur-A-šur [8]na-áš-a-ku-nu-ti

The rings for my hand (and) the package of 1 mina with my seal Puzur-Ašur is bringing to you.

18. KTHahn 26:9, (cf. EL No 124) Memorandum

[5]GÍN KÙ.BABBAR sa-ru-pa-um [8]ša Ší-ša-aḫ-šu-šar [9][a]-na ša-wi-ri-im [10]ša-a-mì-im

Five shekels of refined silver of Sišaḫšušur to buy a bracelet (entrusted to Ennum-Aššur).

19. Kültepe 272:4

ší-na ša-wi-ri-a ad-di-in

I have done two my bracelets.

20. TCL IV,30:11 Letter from Pūšukēn to Ašur-bani, Šalim-Ašur, and Ikunum

[10]...1 MA.NA KÙ.BABBAR [11]ša-wi-ru ša ṣú-ḫa-ar-tim [12]18 GÍN KÙ.GI a-nu-qú-ša [13]2 mi-iḫ-ṣú ḫi-tù u tu-dí-na-[tu]-ša [14]1 MA.NA KÙ.BABBAR ni-is-ḫa-sú DIRIG

The bracelet of the girl (is worth) one mina of silver, her ring – 18 shekels of gold, two *miḫsu*, *ḫittu* and her *tudinatu*; *nisḫatu*-tax is added.

21. TCL XXI, 207:10 Transport contract

[10]...ša-wi-ru [11]ša ṣú-ḫa-ar-tim [12]mì-ma a-nim ni-is-ḫa-su [13]ŠÍ.A ša-du-a-sú [14]ša-bu-u

...the bracelet of the girl – for these all the *nisḫatu*-tax is added, the *šaddu'atu*-tax on it is paid.

tudittu/tudinatu CAD D, 168a *dudittu, tudittu* – „pectoral"; AHw 1365 b – „eine Brustschmuck für Frauen"; Klein, ZA 73, 255ff. – defines it as an object not yet fully defined but in fact is for the term „toogle pin": „pendant, pectoral, toogle pin, brest shield". In this paper, rather: pectoral, kind of necklace.

22. BIN IV 97:14ff. Letter from Ašur-muttabbil to *ša kima jâti*

[14]lu tù-dí-na-tù-ki [15]lu mì-ma i-qa-tí-ka i-ba-ší-u [16]KÙ.BABBAR 1 MA.NA [17]ma-li-a-ma šé-bi-lá-nim

---

[14] Cf. CAD K, 255b *kāsu. GAL ZABAR (UD.KA.BAR)* does not mean the one in command of the bronze, but perheps bowl of bronze, por. WdO III,3, p. 232.

[15] See L. Matouš, in: *Zikir šumim. Assyriological Studies Presented to F. R. Kraus* (Leiden 1982) 269f.

Either your pectorals or whatever is in your hand (up to the amount) of 1 mina of silver send to me.

23. BIN VI, 179:22 Fragment of a letter

[21]x GÍN NA$_4$.ZA.GÌN x GÍN [22]pá-pá-ar-da-li-am [23]qá-qá-da-at tú-di-na-tim

x shekels od lapis lazuli and x shekels of *pappardalium*-stone as *qaqqadatu* – „heads" for the pectorals.[16]

24. CCT I, 31b:2 Notice

...[1]lu KÙ.BABBAR lu kà-sú-um [2]lu tú-dí-na-tùm [3]6 1/2 MA.NA 1 GÍN [4]KÙ.BABBAR... [8]u-šé-ṣí-ú-nim

...either silver or a cup, pectorals (worth) 6 1/2 mina, 1 shekel of silver (all that is brought from Purušhattum).

25. CCT III 29:26, see also No 31, Letter from *ša kima jâti* to Enlil-bani and Ašur-iddin

[25]1/3 MA.NA 1 GÍN KÙ.GI 1/2 GÍN [26]ḫi-tù ù tú-dí-na-tum [27]1 kà-sú-um 1 MA.NA 8 GÍN KÙ.BABBAR... [31]mì-ma a-nim lá ší-bi ip-qí-id-ni-a-tí-ni

1/2 mina 1 shekel of gold, (one) *ḫittu*, (one) pectoral of 1/2 mina and 5 shekels of silver all this was entrusted to the receiver without a witness.

26. CCT IV 24a3'-4' Letter from Taram-Kubi to Innaja; see C. Michel II, No 5[17]

[3'][t]ù-dí-na-tí-ni nu-lá-qí-it a-na KÙ.BABBAR [4'][ší]-im ḫu-sà-re-e a-na È A-lim nu-uš-[ta-qí-il$_5$]

...we have collected our pectorals in silver and given them to the City Hall as the payment for *ḫusaru*.

27. PA 31:4 – W. C. Gwaltney, The Pennsylwania Old Assyrian Texts, HUCA, Supp. 3. 1983 Letter from Enlil-bani to Ab-šalim

...[3]7 GÍN KÙ.BABBAR [4]tú-dí-tam$_4$ ku-nu-ki-a [5]a-na ṣú-ḫa-ar-tim [6]Enna-Sin na-ší

7 shekels of silver, a pectoral (bearing) my seal for the girl, Enna-Sin is carrying.

cf. PA 63 – on a very damaged tablet, w. 4-5 there appears the word *tudittu.*

28. ICK I, 90:28 A letter?

[22]tù-dí-tám ša KÙ.GI u šu[...] [23]ša-pár-tám tú-ka-al

You hold a golden pectoral as pledge.

29. KTS 12:26 Letter from Ašur-nada to Alahum, Šu-Ašur, Zuba, Ili-alum

[25]ša 10 GÍN KÙ.BABBAR sà-ḫi-ir-[tám] [26]lu ṣi-ba-ra-tum lu tú-dí-na-tum

Small ware (*saḫirtu*) worth 10 shekels of silver (consisting of) either *ṣibaratum*, (perhaps: small amount?) or pectorals.

---

[16] *qaqqadat tudinatim* – according to Klein, ZA 73$_{II}$, p. 264: ...als Köpfe von *tudinati*. CAD Q 112b: *qaqqadat* – head tax.

[17] Cf. C. Michel, op.cit., II, p. 18ff.

30. Kültepe c/k 1538:5 Next to *tudittu*, *kasum* and *ḫattum* are mentioned

31. TCL IV 30:13 see No 20 (sub: *šawiru*)

32. TCL XIV 54:4 Report, see EL I, p. 238
4'2 tú-dí-ta-an 1/3 MA.NA KI.LÁ.BI 5'a-na La-ma-sí u A-ḫa-ḫa
Two pectorals weighing 1/3 mina for Lammasi and Aḫaḫa.

33. TCL XXI, 202:15 Transport contract
...15 13 GÍN KÙ.BABBAR tú-dí-na-tam 16a-na ka-li-tí-ni a-ḫa-ma 17 10 GÍN ší-a-tí-ma
A pectoral weighing 13 shekels of silver for our sister-in-law, besides that 10 shekels to her... (all this was entrused to Alaḫum).

34. TCL IV, 30:13 see No 20 (sub: *šawiru*).

IMAGE AND FUNCTION
in early Ninevite 5 administration

Roger J. MATTHEWS
British Institute of Archaeology at Ankara

I dedicate this essay to Doctor Krystyna Szarzyńska in honour of her major contributions to our understanding of early Mesopotamian culture and civilization

1. Introduction

The massive mound of Tell Brak in northeastern Syria has received considerable archaeological attention in the course of the twentieth century. Some of the more famous excavated remains include the Eye Temple of Late Uruk date and the palace of the Akkadian king, Naram Sin, excavated by Max Mallowan in the 1930s. One of the lesser known periods attested at the site, however, is that of Ninevite 5. This period takes it name from level 5 of Max Mallowan's deep sounding, also in the 1930s, at another great north Mesopotamian mound, Nineveh, where coherent assemblages of pottery and seal impressions were recovered. The pottery was marked by distinctive decoration in the form of paint or incised and excised linear designs, while the seal impressions showed connections with other assemblages of the so-called Piedmont Jemdet Nasr or glazed steatite style. These points of contact placed the Ninevite 5 period chronologically within the first half of the third millennium B.C.

In the decades since Mallowan's pioneering excavations at Nineveh, fieldwork across northern Mesopotamia has substantially enhanced our understanding of many aspects of Ninevite 5 culture. We now know that the Ninevite 5 culture was restricted to northern Mesopotamia and that it ran concurrently with, at least, the Early Dynastic 1 period in southern Mesopotamia. Excavations at a range of sites have tended to show that Ninevite 5 settlements were generally not extensive in size, in marked contrast to their contemporary neighbours in southern Mesopotamia, such as the enormous Early Dynastic 1 mounds of Larsa, Uruk, Fara and Al-Hiba. Furthermore, the indications were that Ninevite 5 economic and administrative sophistication was not as developed as that of southern contemporaries. Not a single inscribed Ninevite 5 tablet has been found, for example, although there are a few candidates for simple numerical tablets from Ninevite 5 sites.

It was within this research context that my own excavations at Tell Brak from 1994 to 1996 took as a major focus the desire further to elucidate the nature of Ninevite 5 occupation at this singularly important site. It seemed that if a large and sophisticated Ninevite 5 settlement were to be found in northern Mesopotamia then Tell Brak would be a good place to start the search, at least. During the three seasons of fieldwork conducted under my direction a wide range of Ninevite 5 issues were indeed addressed at Tell Brak, and the results of these investigations have been published in preliminary form in the journal *Iraq* pending preparation of a final report. In this article I am not going to recapitulate all the concerns and issues relating to the Ninevite 5 occupation of the site, but instead I am going to focus on a specific range of material evidence originating from a discrete series of archaeological contexts dating to the early Ninevite 5 period at Tell Brak with the general aim of exploring aspects of administrative sophistication in the early third millennium B.C.

2. Trench HS2 at Tell Brak

Much of our work was concentrated on the large spur, Area HS, at the northwestern edge of the mound. Here eroding deposits were immediately accessible and it quickly became clear that within the bulk of this large spur occupation levels ranging in date from Early Uruk to late third millennium were available for excavation. In all, six trenches were opened along the spur, two of which exposed levels of Ninevite 5 date. In trench HS4 a single-roomed temple of late Ninevite 5 date with associated courtyard was excavated, but here I am going to focus on trench HS2, further down the spur from HS4, where a series of occupation levels of early Ninevite 5 date were explored.

The lowermost phases in trench HS2 comprised a series of mud-brick rooms with carefully plastered floors and an adjacent open area with a large boundary wall. The pottery from these deposits indicates a date at the very beginning of the Ninevite 5 period immediately after the Late Uruk period, that is to say around the start of the third millennium.

3. Trench HS2 Phase 1

Cut through the rooms of the lower phases was a series of pits, originally dug from a now eroded level and then filled with ashy rubbish. After cleaning of the mound's surface these pits were easily visible before excavation. Although not stratigraphically sealed by overlying deposits or architecture, the pits contained a coherent and distinctive assemblage of material items which enable us to assign them with confidence to the early Ninevite 5 period.

Pottery from the phase 1 pits includes a painted chalice bowl, at the western limits of the painted Ninevite 5 spread, fine ribbed cups, large lids and cooking pots with crescentic lugs, all indicative of an early Ninevite 5 date.

The most significant finds from phase 1 came however from just one of the pits, A2004. This pit had a surface area of 2.5 by 2 m and a surviving depth of 0.5 m. The fill of the pit comprised multiple lenses of ashy light brown earth, and it is likely that the pit was dug as a deliberate refuse disposal facility. Small and often fragmentary pieces of unbaked clay were encountered even before cleaning of the surface of the trench. Many of these clay pieces turned out to have impressions made by cylinder seals on their obverse faces, and it is these items which form the main focus of this paper.

4. Clay sealings from pit A2004: image

A total of 143 clay sealings were recovered from pit A2004, including a handful from adjacent surface deposits. 18 of these pieces have no discernible seal impression on their obverse faces. On the obverses of the remaining 125 sealings a total of 17 different cylinder seal impressions are attested, all of which are illustrated in Fig. 1. As can be seen, many of these impressions are extremely fragmentary and it is possible that a few of them belong to the same design. Iconographically, the sealings are of interest. The types of seal impression include curvilinear designs of varying complexity, Figs. 1: 1-8, diamond lattice designs, Figs. 1: 9-11, and a limited range of representational scenes largely featuring simplistic renderings of animals, Figs. 1: 12-17. There appear to be no depictions of humans.

There are few really satisfactory iconographic parallels for the A2004 seal impressions. The Ninevite 5 sealings from Nineveh itself (Collon in press), which also date to early in the Ninevite 5 period, are generally similar, with complex versions of the wheel and ladder designs and more intricately rendered animal scenes. It is noteworthy, again, that no humans are depicted on any of the Nineveh sealings. This reluctance to depict the human figure is in marked contrast to the glyptic repertoire both from the preceding Uruk period in north and south Mesopotamia and from contemporary and later seal designs from Early Dynastic Mesopotamia. Some of the more elaborate curvilinear designs from pit A2004, such as those depicted in Figs. 1: 1-2, bear an arguable resemblance to seal impressions from the Seal Impression Strata at Ur (Legrain 1936), of Early Dynastic I date and therefore at least approximately contemporary with the HS2 deposits. There is also an undeniable relationship between these designs and the so-called Piedmont Jemdet Nasr and glazed steatite styles which occur across a broad band of the upland zones bordering northern and eastern Mesopotamia (Pittman 1994; Marchetti 1996).

In sum, the obverse seal impressions on the A2004 sealings indicate the participation of the early Ninevite 5 inhabitants of Tell Brak within a cultural milieu which spanned much of northern Mesopotamia, with hints or echoes of contacts beyond these immediate environs.

5. Clay sealings from pit A2004: image and function

The study of the reverse faces of clay sealings has grown to be a major focus of research in recent years, and I am not here going to present a detailed account of the development of this field. Suffice to say that it is clear that much useful information on seal usage, in the widest sense, can be gleaned by careful and systematic examination of the reverse faces of clay sealings. This information is based upon study of the often faint impressions made by the objects to which the clay sealings were originally affixed, whether it be the neck of a jar, the lid of a basket, the security mechanism of a store-room door, or some other device.

If we look for functional trends in the A2004 sealings, some interesting points emerge. The quantities of sealings bearing each seal type are as follows:

Seal impression number (as on Fig. 1):

	1	2	3	4	5	6	7	8	9	10	11	12	13	14	15	16	17	None
Qty	39	5	3	4	2	1	4	1	43	2	3	8	1	2	4	2	1	18

Thus, only 2 of the 17 different seal types, numbers 1 and 9 on Fig. 1, occur on large quantities of sealings, 39 and 43 pieces respectively. All the other seal types occur on less than 10 sealings each, the distinctive animal scene, number 12, occurring on 8 pieces in total.

We can look in more detail at the groups of sealings with duplicate seal impressions. Seal type number 1, a complex curvilinear design impressed from a cylinder seal 4.6 cm in height, occurs on 39 separate pieces of clay. Of these, almost all have reverse face impressions of rows of string. In addition, 9 pieces have impressions of curving pegs with grainy markings, suggesting the pegs were made of wood or large reeds (Fig. 2: 1). 15 of the sealings have a flat, moderately smooth surface at right angles to the peg impression, where present, indicating the use of circular pegs stuck into wall surfaces as part of a door closing device. This practice is well attested throughout the Early Dynastic period in Mesopotamia and relates to a mode of door sealing employed to control access to store-rooms containing a range of possible commodities. The seal used on these pieces of clay from pit A2004, and therefore its owner as a participant within an administrative system, thus had a strong connection with store-room door sealing.

The other complex curvilinear seal types, particularly numbers 2 and 3 of Fig. 1, also show a functional connection with strings, pegs and wall surfaces, all probably related to door sealing.

If we look in functional terms at seal type number 9, by contrast, a very different picture emerges. This seal, a simple reticular design with a seal height of

3.1 cm, is attested on 43 pieces of clay. Of these, 19 have clear impressions of basketry and string, showing their use to seal lids of basket containers secured with string (Fig. 2: 2). Another 6 pieces have evidence of having been fixed to pot necks or to other types of container, including one which had been fixed directly to the corrugated surface of a classic early Ninevite 5 cup (Fig. 2: 3) and other vessels (Fig. 2: 4). 11 of the type 9 sealings have impressions from possible pegs with string, occasionally with a level surface from adhesion to a wall of other flat surface. It seems therefore that although the type 9 sealings are largely concerned with the closure of portable containers such as baskets and pots, they are also used in store-room door closure. The few other sealings with reticular seal designs, numbers 10 and 11, all have string impressions only.

Seal number 12 shows a distinctive animal scene, comprising two quadrupeds, perhaps a bovid and a wild goat, with smaller creatures such as a snake and a scorpion/hunting spider and other unidentified motifs above and below the quadrupeds. The seal is small at only 1.7 cm in height and with a circumference of 5.2 cm. The 8 sealings impressed with seal number 12 show evidence of a range of functions. There are 3 pieces from baskets, 1 with fine sacking impressions (Fig. 2: 5) and 2 with marks of a smooth peg with surrounding string (Fig. 2: 6). It seems, then, the type 12 sealings were employed, like the type 9 ones, for sealing both store-room doors and portable containers. The other representational seal types, numbers 13 to 17, also have reverse impressions indicating a range of functions from baskets to door pegs.

6. Conclusions

The overall picture of the A2004 sealings is one of variability, with little rigid correlation between seal type and function. The only strong correlation between image and function is that of seal number 1, the complex curvilinear design, and also the largest seal attested on the sealings. Seal number 1 was used almost exclusively for sealing a store-room door secured with a device of peg and string. The official or administrator in possession of this seal was thus responsible for control over access to one or more store-rooms, with little or no control over access to portable containers.

Other seal owners, by contrast, such as those who owned seals numbers 9 and 12, were responsible mainly for control over access to portable containers, principally baskets but also pots and other unidentified items. On occasion, however, they were empowered to use their seals to secure store-room doors.

We thus have a minimum of 17 seal owners or administrative officials carrying out a range of sealing functions attested by the evidence from pit A2004. These functions include the sealing of store-room doors as well as the securing of unknown commodities within a range of containers. We have no direct evidence of the architectural context within which these sealings originally performed their function. The architecture of this phase does not survive, at least on this part of the site, and we are left only with the pits which were no doubt dug for rubbish disposal. Other items contained within pit A2004 include miniature vessels, clay figurines and many shaped and marked pieces of clay, as well as the early Ninevite 5 pottery already referred to. Disregarding the specifics of the pottery, this assemblage of artefacts has good parallels with other rubbish disposal deposits well known from a range of approximately contemporary sites in southern Mesopotamia, including the Seal Impression Strata at Ur, the 4C88 dump at Jemdet Nasr, and the Id/Ie rubbish dump at Fara (see Matthews 1991 for references to these contexts). The rubbish in pit A2004 is likely therefore to have originated as regular clearings out of unwanted debris from a building of some significance where administrative activities had an important role to play.

Given the nearby presence on the HS spur at Tell Brak of what is clearly a temple in later Ninevite 5 times, also with associated sealings (for this temple and its sealings, see Matthews 1996), it is not too bold to speculate that the A2004 sealings may likewise have performed their functions within the context of ritually-mediated and formalised control over movement of precious commodities as part of the social operation of a small but important temple, a poor but closely related cousin of the much larger-scale ritual centres attested by the evidence from contemporary Early Dynastic I south Mesopotamia.

References

Collon, D., *The Ninevite 5 seal impressions from Nineveh*, in H. Weiss (ed.) *The origins of north Mesopotamian civilization* (New Haven, Yale University), in press.

Legrain, L., 1936. *Ur excavations* III. *Archaic seal impressions*. London: British Museum.

Marchetti, N., 1996. *The Ninevite 5 glyptic of the Khabur region and the chronology of the Piedmont style motifs*. BaghMitt 27, 81-115.

Matthews, R. J., 1991. *Fragments of officialdom from Fara*. Iraq 53, 1-15.

Matthews, R. J., 1996. *Excavations at Tell Brak*, 1996. Iraq 58, 65-77.

Pittman, H., 1994. *The glazed steatite glyptic style*. Berlin: BBVO.

List of figures (all figures are at scale 1:1)

Fig. 1:1 Seal impression number 1, occurring on 39 sealings.
Fig. 1:2 Seal impression number 2, occurring on 5 sealings.
Fig. 1:3 Seal impression number 3, occurring on 3 sealings.
Fig. 1:4 Seal impression number 4, occurring on 4 sealings.
Fig. 1:5 Seal impression number 5, occurring on 2 sealings.
Fig. 1:6 Seal impression number 6, occurring on 1 sealing.
Fig. 1:7 Seal impression number 7, occurring on 4 sealings.
Fig. 1:8 Seal impression number 8, occurring on 1 sealing.
Fig. 1:9 Seal impression number 9, occurring on 43 sealings.
Fig. 1:10 Seal impression number 10, occurring on 2 sealings.
Fig. 1:11 Seal impression number 11, occurring on 3 sealings.
Fig. 1:12 Seal impression number 12, occurring on 8 sealings.
Fig. 1:13 Seal impression number 13, occurring on 1 sealing.
Fig. 1:14 Seal impression number 14, occurring on 2 sealings.
Fig. 1:15 Seal impression number 15, occurring on 4 sealings.
Fig. 1:16 Seal impression number 16, occurring on 2 sealings.
Fig. 1:17 Seal impression number 17, occurring on 1 sealing.

Fig. 2:1 Sealing A2004:2:18. On obverse: impression of seal number 1. On reverse: impressions of curved object with string and level flat surface.
Fig. 2:2 Sealing A2004:2:51. On obverse: impression of seal number 9. On reverse: impressions of basketry and string.
Fig. 2:3 Sealing A2004:17:7. On obverse: impression of seal number 9. On reverse: impression of rim and corrugated neck of early Ninevite 5 cup.
Fig. 2:4 Sealing A2004:2:61. On obverse: impression of seal number 9. On reverse: impression of pot profile from rim to lower neck, covered in sacking and wound with string.
Fig. 2:5 Sealing A2004:2:9. On obverse: impression of seal number 12. On reverse: impressions of fine sacking and string.
Fig. 2:6 Sealing A2004:2:5. On obverse: impression of seal number 12. On reverse: impressions of smooth curving peg, string and level flat surface.

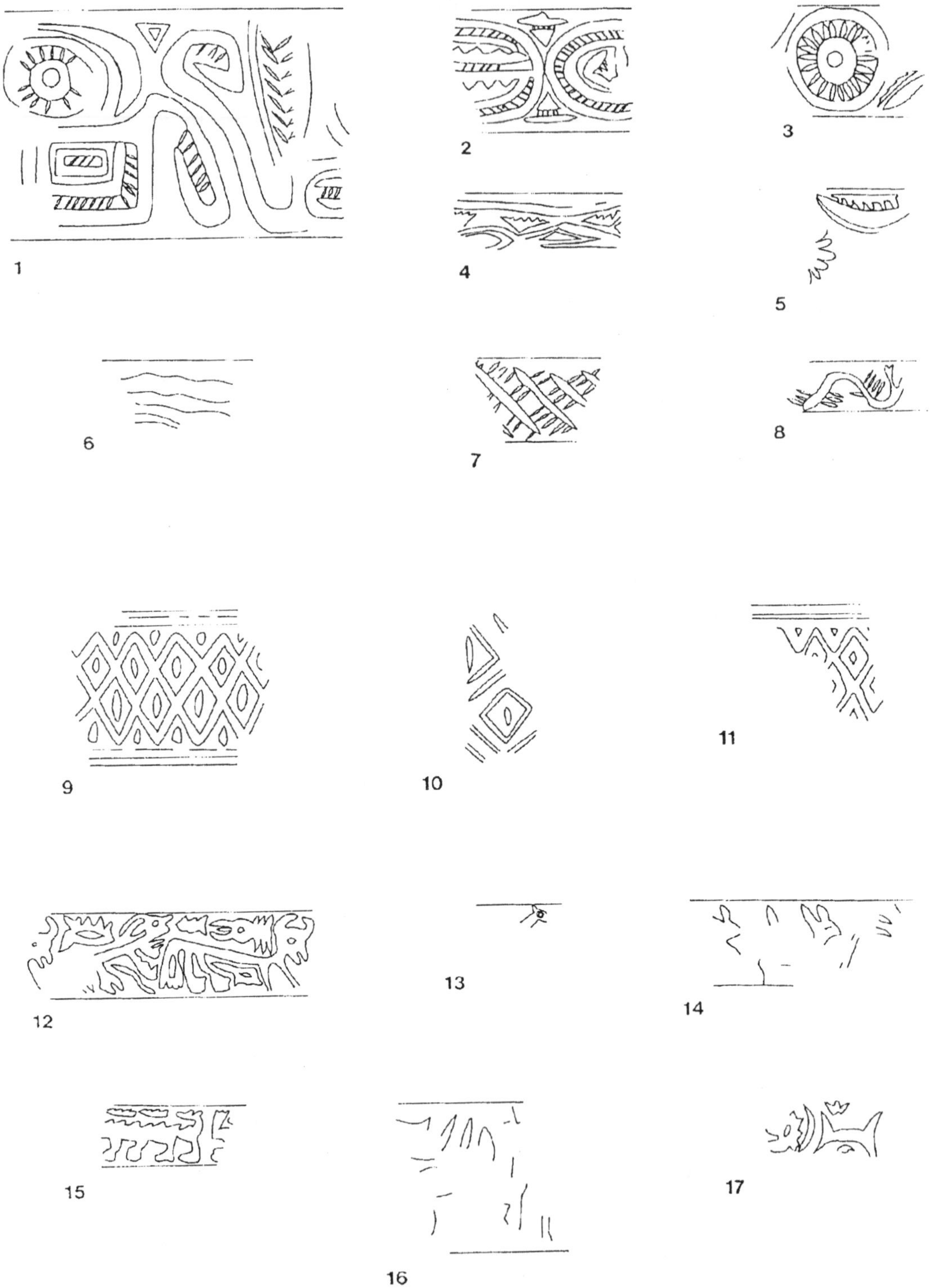

Fig. 1

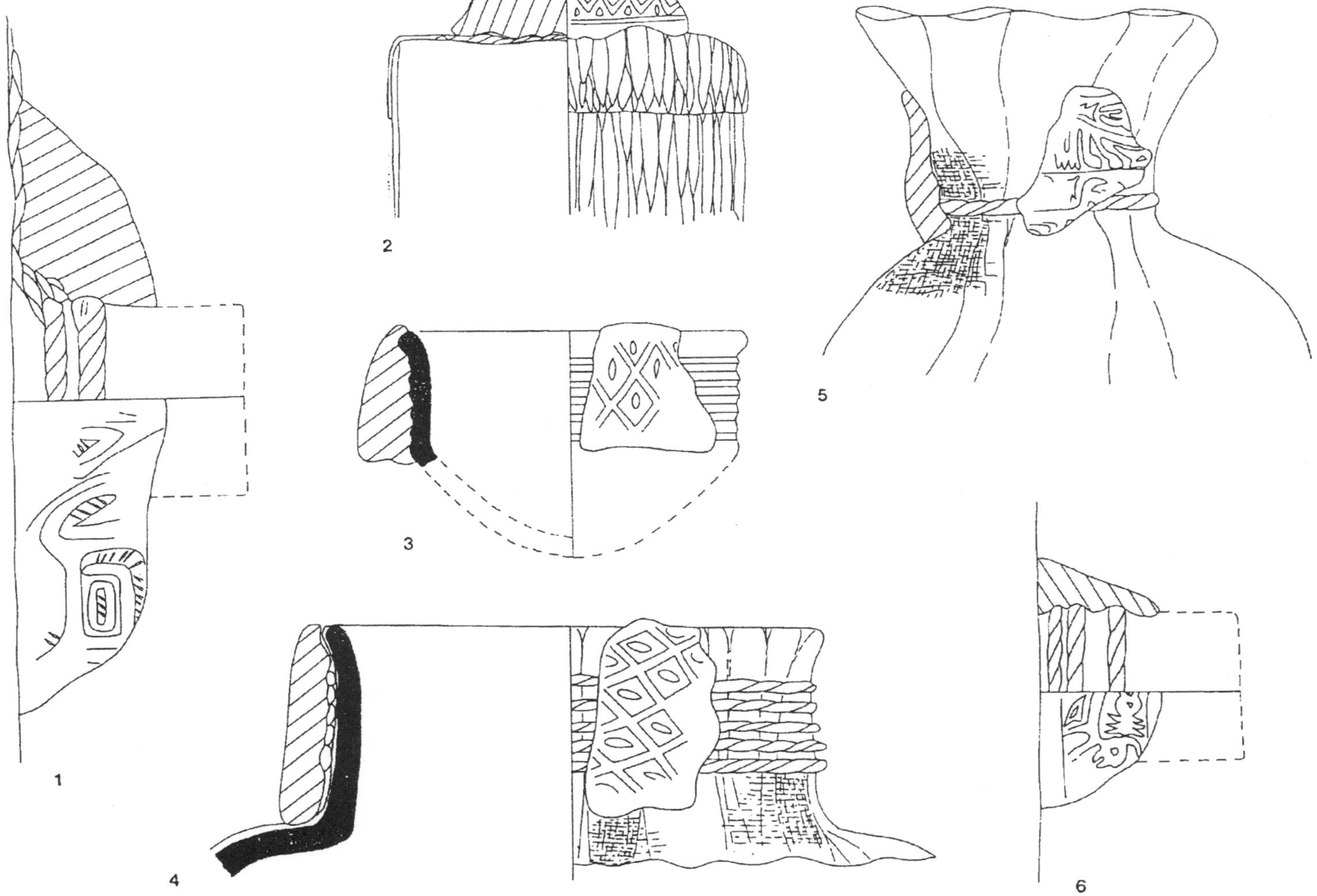

Fig. 2

LITERATURE AS A SOURCE OF LEXICAL INSPIRATION: SOME NOTES ON A HYMN TO THE GODDESS INANA[1]

Piotr Michałowski
The University of Michigan, Ann Arbor

1. Introduction

A decade ago Miguel Civil published a brief article under the fascinating title: *Feeding Dumuzi's Sheep: The Lexicon as a Source of Literary Inspiration.*[2] Civil drew attention to a device he described as „enumeration" in which „a text may consist mainly of a listing of terms of a lexical set."[3] One text that contains a long set of words linked in semantic sets, albeit in ways different than Civil had in mind when he wrote that article, is the Old Babylonian Sumerian language hymn to the goddess Inana, known by its opening line as *Inin ša gura.*[4] Although one of its lines ascribes the composition to Enheduana, daughter of Sargon of Akkad, there is no direct evidence to support this, and it is possible that the hymn was composed sometime during the Old Babylonian period.[5] This poem includes a long section in which certain characteristics of the goddess are listed, in the form of chained, semantically related nouns, followed by the refrain „are your domain, O Inana." This, for example, we learn in lines 119 through 124 that:

„To destroy, build up, raising and lowering are your domain, O Inana,

---

[1] This small contribution is offered with affection to Dr. Krystyna Szarzyńska; although it does not deal with archaic Sumerian subject matters, it does have some bearing on the literary portrayal of Inana, who has been the subject of important work by Dr. Szarzyńska. I would like to thank Miguel Civil for his comments and suggestions on an earlier version of his paper.

[2] Pp. 37-56 in F. Rochberg-Halton (ed). *Language, Literature, and History: Philological and Historical Studies Presented to Erica Reiner* (New Haven 1987).

[3] Ibid., 37.

[4] Åke W. Sjöberg, *in-nin šà-gur$_4$-ra: A Hymn to the Goddess Inanna by the* en-*Priestess Enheduanna*, ZA 65 (1975) 161-253.

[5] See M. Civil, *Les limites de l'information textuelle* in T. Barrelet (ed.), *L'archeologie de l'Iraq du début de l'époque néolithique à 333 avant notre ère: perspectives et limites de l'interpretation anthropologique des documents.* (Paris 1980) p. 229.

To turn a man into a woman, and a woman into man are your domain, O Inana,

Attractiveness, sexual appeal, to have property and a house full of gods are your domain, O Inana,

Profit, commerce, trade, and capital gain are your domain, O Inana,

Business, earnings, loss and deficit are your domain, O Inana,

Information, instruction, inspection, close inspection and approval are yours, O Inana."

This kind of „enumeration" is a poetic device that exploits broad selection of Sumerian vocabulary, combined on the basis of various types of semantic association.

2. Kelsey Museum 89404

In order to shed some light on one aspect of the history and impact of this type of composition, I would like to focus here on two lines of text, in part as a pretext to publish a new source for the reconstruction of *Inin ša gura*. The new tablet is housed in the collection of the Kelsey Museum of Archaeology at the University of Michigan in Ann Arbor, and is published here by kind permission of my friend and colleague, Prof. Sharon Herbert, the director of the museum.[6] The Kelsey tablet is an oblong rectangular exercise text with a cuneiform text on the obverse and a blank reverse.[7] It is inscribed with two lines from the Sumerian Inana hymn *Inin ša gura* with Akkadian translations. Nothing is known about the provenance of the object, but one can safely state, on the basis of the shape, content, and layout of the writing, that it is not from Nippur or Ur, the two cities that have been the main sources of Old Babylonian Sumerian school texts. The date of the tablet is uncertain. On general paleographic grounds one is tempted to ascribe it to the Old Babylonian period: the use of mimation would support this supposition, but some of the sign values in the Akkadian version point to a later time. The use of *šá* and *pal* is rare in OB; the former only encountered at that time when used for the independent pronoun,[8] and *kit* is not attested in Akkadian before the Kassite period. This demonstrates once again how difficult it is to date Sumerian literary texts on the basis of paleography.

[6] The tablet was discovered and identified by Brian Keck, who authored a catalog entry on this object in the exhibition catalog edited by Marti Lu Allen and T. Keith Dix, *The Beginning of Understanding: Writing in the Ancient World* (Ann Arbor 1991).

[7] The tablet measures 8.4x4.6x2.4 cm.

[8] See W. von Soden and W. Röllig, *Das akkadische Syllabar* (Rome 1976).

The oblong shape of the tablet suggest that the tablet, as noted above, does not come from Old Babylonian Nippur or Ur, although such tablets were in use in other Southern sites such as Uruk.[9] At least two similar tablets from Babylon have been published and one, a bilingual excerpt from a Sargon tale, is quite similar to the Kelsey tablet.[10] This type of practice text became standard in later Kassite times at Nippur, but all the examples I have seen are smaller in size. In summary, one might suggest that the tablet is early Kassite, most probably from northern Babylonia.

The two lines on the tablet, which correspond to lines 158 and 159 of the composite edition, read as follows:

1. ba-an-gi lul zi bi-ri-IG / níg kúr di-di ᵈinin za-a-kam
na-pal-ti kit-ti sà-ar-tim gu-un-nu-⸢ṣu⸣ me bi ri k[a?] x [...]
2. a-⸢tar-lá-lá⸣ níg kúr di-di zú-bir₉ / pi-il-lá dugud-da ᵈinin ⸢za⸣-a-⸢kam⸣
⸢*šu-ta-ṣù*⸣*-ú qá-be-e šá-ni-ti ṣu-*⸢*uḫ-ḫu*⸣ *qù-ul-lu k*[*a*]*-b*[*a*ˀ*-tu*]

The only other source that contains both lines is the Nippur tablet Q (CBS 2357 = HAV 20). Line 159 is also attested in the bilingual Harmal text R (IM 51176 = *Sumer* 13 [1957] pl. 3). In the commentary that follows, all the versions, which, to reiterate, come from different places, have been lined up for easy comparison.[11] For reasons that will become clear, we shall deal with these two lines in reverse order.

Line 159. As noted by A. Cavigneaux, this line is quoted in the first five lines of tablet II of the lexical series erimhuš = *anantu*[12] To make matters simpler, I have included this as one of the „sources" for the line in the correlation provided here, where it is designated as EA. The new manuscript of Erimhuš II from Uruk, is entered separately as EAu.[13]

KM	a-⸢tar-lá-lá⸣ níg kúr di-di	zú-bir₉ / pi-il-lá dugud-da ᵈinin ⸢za⸣-a-⸢kam⸣
Q	a-tar-lá-lá níg kúr du₁₁-du₁₁	zú-bir₉ dugud (ᵈinin za-a-kam)

[9] On oblong school tablets see my remarks in *An Old Babylonian Literary Fragment Concerning Kassites*, AION 41 (1981) 385-389.
[10] VS 24 38 and 75 (Sargon text). A photo of the latter has been published by Joan Goodnick Westenholtz, *Legends of the Kings of Akkade.* (Winona Lake 1997) p. 382.
[11] For practical reasons the Sumerian and Akkadian lines have been entered separately. KM designates the Kesley Museum tablet.
[12] P. 3 in A. Cavigneaux et al. (eds.), *The Series Erim-ḫuš = anantu and An-ta-gál = šaqû* (Rome 1985) (hereafter MSL 17).
[13] Egbert von Weiher, *Uruk : Spätbabylonische Texte aus dem Planquadrat* U 18. Teil IV. Ausgrabungen in Uruk-Warka. Endberichte; Bd. 12 (Mainz 1993) no 187, lines x+1-4. I give only the Sumerian, as the Akkadian translation adds nothing new. Note also a-tar-lál, the incipit of tablet II in the catalog of lexical texts, in no 186 line 15 of the same volume. For practical reasons EA is the composite text from MSL, the Sumerian version of which is primarily based on an unpublished Nippur text from Istanbul.

R a-ta-ar-la-e ni$_5$-in-kur du-tu su-li pu-ul-la-ad-gu-ud ^{d}inin za-a-kam
EA [ ]/ [ ]-kúr /du$_{11}$-du$_{11}$/ zú-bir$_9$ pi-il-lá dugud
Eau [a]-tar-lá-lá / níg kúr di-di / zú$^{bi-ir}$-bir$_9$ / pil^{pi-il}-lá [á]$^{du-gu-ud}$dugud

KM ⌈*šu-ta-ṣú*⌉*-ú qá-be-e šá-ni-ti ṣu-*⌈*uḫ-ḫu*⌉ *qú-ul-lu k*[*a*]*-b*[*a?-tu*]
EA [*šu-t*]*e-ṣu-ú* / [*q*]*a-ab šá-ni-tú / ṣu-uḫ-ḫu / qu-lu-lu / kab-du-du*
R *šu-te-ṣu-ú-um e-pé-eš na-mu-tim ṣú-ḫu-um qa-la-lu ù ka-ba-tum ku-ma eštar*

The Kelsey text provides a much better Akkadian translation for the line and, moreover, one that is closer to the later lexical series than the version from Tell Harmal. The main difference between the two is found in the Akkadian rendering of níg kúr du$_{11}$-du$_{11}$. The Harmal version has *ēpeš namūtim*, „to joke", but the Kelsey tablet has a completely different rendering, one that is almost identical to the much later entry in the lexical text. Or, perhaps better, „to behave in a shoking manner", possibly conceived of as a specific behavior associated with the cult of Inana. See now B. Groneberg, *Namûtu ša Ištar*: „Das Transvestiesschauspiel der Ištar", NABU 1997, 64-66.

A word should be said about the reading of the Sumerian KA.NE, rendered here as zú-bir$_9$ (NE). As B. Landsberger already pointed out in MSL XI 119, the second sign in this work must be read either as /bar/ or /bir/, as evidenced in Lu IV 244a (MSL XII 136): [zú-bir$_9$-bir$_9$]-re = *mu-ṣi-iḫ-ḫu*. Solely on the basis of the syllabic writing su-li of the Harmal source of this line, B. Alster (RA 67 [1973] 110) proposed the reading zú-li$_9$-(r), which has gained currency.[14] This is unlikely, as it would be the only Sumerian word built on the pattern CvC to contain two liquid consonants. The gloss bi-ir in the new Uruk source for Erimhuš II from Uruk confirms Landsberger's reading.

Line 158
KM ba-an-gi lul zi bi-ri-ig / níg kúr di-di ^{d}inin za-a-kam
na-pal-ti kit-ti sà-ar-tim gu-un-nu-⌈*ṣu*⌉me bi ri k[a?] x [...]
Q ba-an-gi$_4$ lul zi bi-ri-ig níg-á-zi du$_{11}$-du$_{11}$ (^{d}inin za-a-kam)

The new source appears to have a few words at the end of the Akkadian rendition that do not have any counterpart in the Sumerian. I am unable to restore this part of the line.

ba-an-gi$_4$ posed a problem for the editor of the text, but in PSD B 16 the word was correctly analyzed as a noun derived from a frozen verbal form on the pattern ba-an-R. Although no Akkadian lexical equivalent was known, the

---

[14] The final /r/ is also documented by zú-bir$_9$-bir$_9$-ra in *Home of the Fish* 141, cited by Alster.

authors of the dictionary surmised that it would have to be connected with *apālu*, „to answer." The new rendering of ba-an-gi$_4$ as *napaltu* confirms that supposition, supporting their translation, „to sneer at a response that is false or true and to be violent (are yours, oh Inana!)".

bi-ri-IG is translated here by *gunnuṣu*, literally, „to constantly wrinkle one's nose". The Akkadian verb has not been hitherto attested in OB or MB and the only lexical attestation of the correspondence between the Sumerian and Akkadian comes from erimhuš tablet II 90-91 (MSL 17 31):

bi-ri-IG = *gu-un-nu-ṣu*
níg-á-zi = *ga-na-ṣu*
and, in the same series tablet IV 104 (MSL 17 62)
[b]i-ri-IG = *a-an-ṣu*

The relationship between the two first entries is not clear, and one may suggest that they actually derive from a version of *Inin ša gura*, as the precedent for this is provided by line 159. Unfortunately, the only preserved sources for these lines are from first millennium Mesopotamia, and they are not attested in the earlier Boghazköy versions.

This is not the only strong connection between the Inana hymn and the lexical series Erimhuš. Many of the words used in the hymn are listed there (including the rare word erim-huš) and at least two other direct quotations may be cited. Line 157 of *Inin ša gura* reads:

eme-sig inim a-ša-an-ga-ra ka é-gal kúr-du$_{11}$-ga dah du$_{11}$-du$_{11}$ ^{d}inin za-a-kam

This appears in the following manner in Erimhuš I 280-283:

280 [em]e-sig = *kar-ṣu*
281 a-ša-an-ga-ra = *taš-ri-it-tú*
282 ka é-gal = *šil-la-tú*
283 kúr-du$_{11}$-ga = *tu-uš-šú*

More complex is the relationship between line 162 of the Inana hymn and a section of the Boghazköy version of Erimhuš that does not appear to have been incorporated into the first millennium redaction of the lexical text. Once again, the only Mesopotamian witnesses for the literary composition are Q and R. The earlier Anatolian version, attested only in one copy (KBo 1 44+), is cited from the text provided in MSL, which can be consulted for minor details.

162 Q ù-ma níg-x-x im-ba-sur igi-lib ù nu-ku
R ù-ma ni$_5$-pa-hu$^?$-ur ip-pa-su-ur i-gi-li-ib-bi ù nu-ku ^{d}inanna za-kam
ir-ne-tum re-du-um ra-i-bu di-li-ip-tum ù la ṣa-la-lu ku-ma eštar

In Åke Sjöberg's the line means: „Triumph, pursuit, the *imbasur* disease, sleeplessness and restlessness are yours, Inana."

This is undoubtedly the source of Erimhuš Bogh. A i 39-47 (MSL 17, 103-4), a Sumerian-Akkadian-Hittite trilingual:[15]

39 [x]-x-sur = *za-a-bu* = *ḫal-ḫal-x-wa-liš*
40 x-x-x-hul = *ḫa-a-lu* = *ú-i-wi*$_5$*-iš-kat-tal-la-aš*
41 ⌈igi⌉-lib(LUL.A) = *dá-la-pu* = *ar-ri-ia-a-u-wa-ar*
42 igi-lib-kúr = *la-a ṣa-la-lu* = *Ú-UL še-eš-ki-ia-u-wa-ar*
43 [Á]Š.SAG = *al-pu* = *šar-ḫu-un-ta-al-liš*
44 [á]š-dah = *ar-ta-ti-el-lu* = *ka-aš-ta-an-za*
45 [á]š-dah-di = [*ka*]*r*-⌈*ri-ru*⌉= *za-ap-pí*-⌈*at*⌉*-tal-la-aš*
46 ù-ma = *en-ni*-⌈*id-du*⌉= [x x x x]*-ia-u-wa-ar*
47 ù-ma = *kat-ti-lu* = *ar-m*[*a-li*]*ia-u-wa-ar*
48 [i]gi-huš = *né-kél-m*[*u-u*] = *tar*-⌈*gul*⌉*-li-ia-u-wa-ar*

It is clear that at some point the connection between the hymn and the lexical text was lost; lines 43-45 were inserted and 46 moved to its present position.

3. Discussion

The relationship between *Inin ša gura* and the lexical series Erimhuš established above raises many new issues about Mesopotamian literary history. The Kelsey tablet appears to be early Kassite in date and adds to our knowledge about the manuscript tradition of *Inin ša gura*. In his standard edition of the composition Åke Sjöberg was able to utilize thirty manuscripts. All but one were Old Babylonian: twenty-three monolingual Sumerian tablets from Nippur, one Sumerian text of unknown provenance, and six bilingual versions from Tell Harmal. One Nippur text, in bilingual format, seems to come from Kassite times.[16] There is another unpublished bilingual duplicate from Nippur, which appears to come from the same period.[17] The composition is mentioned in line 40 of the Old Babylonian „Louvre Catalog", undoubtedly from Nippur, but is otherwise not attested from any other excavated site.[18] The only indication that this Inana hymn was known outside Nippur and Shaduppum (Tell

[15] I have resisted the temptation to restore the Sumerian column on the basis of the hymn, as I cannot collate the original tablet for the present article.
[16] ZA 65 (1975) 161 and 168.
[17] CBS 15203. I am grateful to Miguel Civil for providing me with a photo of this tablet.
[18] See, most recently, E. Flückiger-Hawker, *Der 'Louvre-Catalog' TCL 15 28 und sumerische na-ru*

Harmal) is provided, at the present time, by a Yale collection tablet of unknown origin, by an entry in an unprovenanced literary catalogue, and by the text published here.[19]

The history of the other text we have been discussing here, the lexical series Erimhuš, is equally complex. The majority of the preserved manuscripts of the five tablet canonical recension date from the first millennium, including Seleucid copies. The earliest tablet of the canonical version appears to be a Middle Assyrian copy of the third tablet from Assur.[20] The older history of the composition is represented by approximately twenty cuneiform tablets and fragments from the Hittite capital of Boghazköy and one fragment from Ugarit.[21] It is interesting that the Anatolian copies covered only the material that was part of the first two tablets of the series, and the tablet from Ugarit belonged to tablet 1, leading to the conclusion that the early second millennium redaction of the series may have been limited to the equivalent of this part of the later version.[22] The second millennium Anatolian copies of Mesopotamian lexical texts, including Erimhuš, date from the period of the late Hittite „Empire," that is roughly from the years 1370-1185 B.C.[23] The literary material from Ugarit can now be dated more precisely, as it is becoming clear that most such texts found at Ras Shamra were written during the last quarter of the 12th century and were preserved when the city was destroyed around 1185 B.C.[24] The „Western" late second millennium literary texts of Mesopotamian origin, represented by the tablets from Ugarit, Boghazköy, Emar and other sites are known to us primarily in copies from the 12th century, and thus they overlap temporally with the so-called library of Tiglath-pileser I (1114-1076) from Assur.[25] This overlap is misleading, however, since the „western" texts were not copies of contemporary works from Babylonia and Assyria, but represented a frozen, more ancient offshoot of Old Babylonian literary traditions.[26] In Babylonia there is no trace of Erimhuš in the numerous 17th century texts from Nippur and elsewhere, nor it is to be found among the later Old

---

[19] Mark E. Cohen, *Literary Texts from the Andrews University Archeological Museum*, RA 70 (1976) 131, line 1.

[20] MSL 17 45.

[21] Edited separately by H. Güterbock and M. Civil in MSL 17 97-128. The Ugarit source (U) is included in the MSL edition of tablet 1.

[22] MSL 17 4.

[23] G. Beckman, *Mesopoamians and Mesopotamian Learning at Hattuša*, JCS 35 (1983) 101.

[24] A.-S. Dalix, *Examples de bilinguisme à Ougarit. 'Iloumilkou: la double identité d'un scribe*, in F. Briquel-Chatonnet (ed.), *Mosaïque de languages, mosaïque culturelle. Le bilinguisme dans le Proche-Orient ancien* (Paris 1996) pp. 81-90. See also D. Pardee, JAOS 117 (1997) 376 n. 2.

[25] The most recent discussion of these tablets is found in Olof Pedersén, *Archives and Libraries in the City of Assur. A Survey of the Material from the German Excavations.* Part 1. (Uppsala, 1985) pp. 31-42.

[26] See the remarks of M. Civil, *The Texts from Meskene-Emar*, Aula Orientalis 6 (1989) 5.

Babylonian tablets from Sippar, Babylon, and Kish. The two tablet recension of the lexical series must therefore be dated to early Kassite times, early enough to make it to the West, but before the date of the Middle Assyrian libraries from Assur that already included Tablet III, which apparently was not part of the earlier redaction. The Inana hymn, which did not survive into the late Mesopotamian literary corpus, must have also been used during the early Kassite period, and it was at this time that it served as one of the sources for the scribe or scribes who created the original version of the lexical series Erimhuš. Since only certain lines that were so used were, it is possible that only an excerpt was available to the compiler of Erimhuš.

The Kelsey text has provided an excuse for a short discussion of the relationship between a bilingual Sumero-Akkadian hymn and one of the secondary lexical texts that were compiled in the second millennium. Compositions of this type, primarily Erimhuš, Antagal, and *Nabnitu* have been taken to be „Akkado-Sumerian indexes to the lists Ea, Diri, Izi, Kagal, and the like".[27] This is undoubtedly the case, but the evidence presented here demonstrates that other sources were used as well.

[27] M. Civil, *Lexicography* in S. J. Lieberman (ed.), *Sumerological Studies in honor of Thorkild Jacobsen* (Chicago 1976). p. 126.

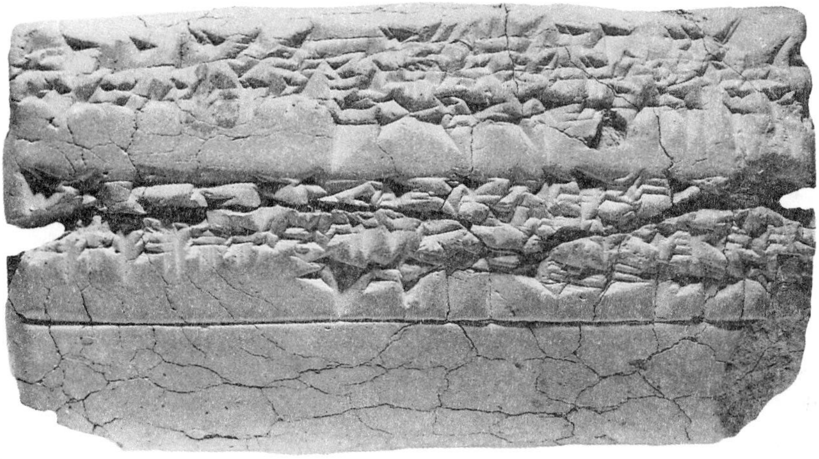

AUF DER SUCHE NACH DEN SIEGREICHEN WAFFEN DES WETTERGOTTES VON ḪALAB IN KLEINASIEN

Maciej Popko

Die Verwandtschaftsbande zwischen dem anatolischen Teššub und dem Wettergott von Ḫalab werden schon lange wahrgenommen[1], aber eingehende Behandlungen dieses Thema stehen nach wie vor aus. Der Kult des Teššub verbreitete sich in Kleinasien in mittelhethitischer Periode infolge der politischen, kulturellen und religiösen Wandlungen, die u.a. durch den Zustrom der Hurriter verursacht wurden. Alles zeigt darauf, daß die hurritische Bevölkerung meistens aus Kizzuwatna und Nordsyrien ankam. Sie hat ihren höchsten Gott, den Teššub von Ḫalab, nach Anatolien in dieser Gestalt mitgebracht, in der er damals in Syrien verehrt wurde. Dieser Gott, mit der Göttin Ḫebat als Gemahlin, den Bergen Nanni und Ḫazzi und anderen Attributen syrischer Herkunft, ist zum Hauptgott des offiziellen Pantheons des hethitischen Staates geworden. Die Umstände dieses Ereignisses sind noch unklar. Trotz aller Bedenken erscheint es sehr wahrscheinlich, daß in jener Zeit eine Gruppe der Hurriter die Macht in Ḫattuša ergriffen hat, was sich auch in der Sphäre der Religion widerspiegeln mußte[2]. Die eminente Stellung dieses Gottes im offiziellen Kult wird durch zahlreiche Texte beleuchtet. Sehr lehrreich ist in dieser Hinsicht KUB 18.22 + KUB 22.15 (Orakelprotokoll), in dem (Vs. 1f. und 4) Ḫattuša als Stadt des Wettergottes von Ḫalab bezeichnet wird[3].

Das Bild des Gottes hat sich unter dem Einfluß anatolischer Vorstellungen etwas verändert; z.B. wurde jetzt der kilikische Gott Šarrum(m)a zum Sohn des Teššub und Ḫebat, wobei seine Adoption wohl noch in Kizzuwatna erfolgt hat. Anstelle des Tašmišu tritt in hethitischen Texten der Gott Šuwalijaz als Bruder und Begleiter des Teššub auf[4]. Nach diesem neuen Muster konnten verschiedene Lokalformen des Teššub sowie auch Wesenszüge anderer Wettergötter modifiziert werden.

Zu den aus Nordsyrien mitgebrachten Attributen des Teššub sollten auch seine siegreichen Waffen gehören, die in der Legende vom Wettergott von Ḫalab

---

[1] Vgl. H. Klengel, *Der Wettergott von Ḫalab*, JCS 19 (1965) 87-93; G. Wilhelm, *Grundzüge der Geschichte und Kultur der Hurriter* (Darmstadt 1982) 71; V. Haas, *Geschichte der hethitischen Religion* (Leiden-New York-Köln 1994) 332f., 554f.

[2] S. schon H. G. Güterbock, *The Hurrian Element in the Hittite Empire*, CHM 2 (1954) 386ff.

[3] Zu diesem Text s. V. Haas, AoF 23 (1996) 78ff. (mit Literaturangaben).

[4] Zu diesem Gott s. zuletzt E. Neu, *Das hurritische Epos der Freilassung* I (Wiesbaden 1996 = StBoT 32) 244f.

eine große Rolle spielen. Wie bekannt, wurde diesem Gott in der Machtperiode von Jamḫad infolge der theologischen Bemühungen der Mythos vom Kampf gegen das Meer zugeeignet, der an der Meerküste enstehen mußte[5]. Dann wurden die Waffen (^{GIŠ}TUKUL$^{\text{ḪI.A}}$), mit denen der Gott das Meer geschlagen haben sollte, zu seinem wichtigen Attribut. In den Zeiten des Zimri-Lim wurden sie nach Terqa geschickt, wo sie im Tempel des Dagan als Krönungsinsignien aufbewahrt waren[6]. Diese Waffen werden in einem ugaritischen Mythos als zwei Keulen wohl ungewöhnlicher Konstruktion beschrieben, und es liegt die Vermutung nahe, daß auf einigen Siegeln, die wahrscheinlich aus Aleppo stammen, der lokale Wettergott gerade mit diesen Keulen dargestellt wird[7].

In der kleinasiatischen Ikonographie erscheint Teššub nur mit einer Streitkeule in der Hand[8], und dieses Prinzip findet seine Entsprechung in einigen Texten, die die kultische Ausstattung verschiedener Tempel schildern. Als Beispiel kann KUB 38.2 Vs. II 8ff. dienen: „Wettergott des Himmels, Statuette eines Mannes, goldbelegt, sitzend, in der rechten Hand hält er eine Keule (^{GIŠ}*ḫattala-*), in der linken Hand hält er das „Heil"-Symbol aus Gold, auf zwei Bergen, Mannesbildern..."[9]. Die Erwähnung der zwei Berge, scil. Nanni und Ḫazzi, läßt in diesem Gott den anatolischen Teššub erkennen. Der Text ist leider beschädigt, und die Angaben zur Lage seines Tempels fehlen.

Gut bekannt ist die kultische Ausstattung eines Tempels des Teššub, der wegen der Anwesenheit der Kultbilder der gestorbenen Könige als Ort des dynastischen Kultes zu deuten und folglich in der Hauptstadt, wohl auf Büyükkale zu suchen ist. Die Anzahl der Textfragmente, die unter CTH 660 gebucht sind und Kultzeremonien im Adyton dieses Tempels beschreiben, hat sich zuletzt vermehrt infolge der Veröffentlichung von KBo 39 und VS N.F. XII. Die betreffenden Texte sind Gegenstand der Untersuchung von D. Groddek, so beschränken wir uns hier auf das Wichtigste für unser Thema. Unter den beopferten Kultobjekten, die die Ausstattung des Adytons des Teššub bilden, wird ^{GIŠ}TUKUL genannt, vgl. KUB 10.11+ KBo 24.89 Vs. III 19', Rs. IV 18 (Dupl. KBo 39.89 Rs. IV 3'), KBo 39.86 Vs. II 8', KBo 2.29 Vs. 5', KBo 2.30 Vs. 9, KBo 39.88 Vs. II 5' und VS N.F. XII Nr. 2 Vs. I 6' (^{GIŠ}TUKUL DINGIR^{LIM}). ^{GIŠ}TUKUL wird gelegentlich als „Keule", meistens jedoch allgemein als „Waffe" gedeutet[10]. Die Keule als Attribut des Teššub bleibt in Übereinstim-

---

[5] S. J.-M. Durand, *Le mythologème du combat entre le Dieu de l'Orage et la Mer en Mésopotamie*, MARI 7 (1993) 41ff.

[6] J.-M. Durand, a. a. O. 52ff.

[7] Vgl. M. Popko, *Zum Wettergott von Ḫalab*, AoF 25 (1998) 119ff. (mit früherer Literatur).

[8] Wie z. B. auf dem Relief von Yazılıkaya bzw. auf dem Siegel des Ini-Tešub (K. Bittel, *Les Hittites*, Paris 1976, Abb. 182).

[9] L. Jakob-Rost, *Zu den hethitischen Bildbeschreibungen*, I. Teil, MIO 8 (1961) 176.

[10] Zu diesem Begriff s. zuletzt R. H. Beal, AoF 15 (1988) 269ff.

mung mit der anatolischen Ikonographie, aber zur diskutierten Textgruppe zählt wohl auch ein kleines, schlecht erhaltenes Textfragment KBo 39.90[11], nach dem ^{GIŠ}TUKUL$^{\text{ḪI.A}}$ „Waffen" (Rs.$^{?}$ IV 6') als Kultgegenstände beopfert werden. Höhstwahrscheinlich handelt es sich in allen obigen Fällen um einen und denselben Kultraum, es ist also nicht auszuschließen, daß in der Schreibung ^{GIŠ}TUKUL (ohne Pluraldeterminativ) eine Abkürzung vorliegt und sich unter dieser Beziechnung in der Tat die siegreichen Waffen des Teššub verbergen.

Im jh. Textfragment KBo 17.85 findet sich ^{GIŠ}TUKUL (Z. 4') unter den beopferten Kultobjekten, die sicherlich mit einem Wettergott in Verbindung stehen. Der Text erinnert teilweise an die vorher genannten Urkunden, aber seine Einordnung bietet Schwierigkeiten – ähnlich wie eine Identifizierung seines Hauptgottes. Sein anderes Attribut ist der (Last-)Wagen (Z.2' ^{GIŠ}MAR.GÍD.DA$^{\text{ḪI.A}}$). Das Wort ist hier, wie übrigens öfter der Fall, mit dem Pluralzeichen geschrieben, doch geht es offenbar um nur eine Karre mit Querbalkenrädern, die in Kleinasien wohlbekannt ist. Dieses Gefährt ist ebenfalls ein Element der Ausstattung des oben erwähnten Adytons des Teššub (vgl. z.B. KUB 10.11+ Vs. III 21', Rs. IV 18), und seine Verknüpfung mit diesem Gott wird durch den Lied von Ullikummi bestätigt. Andererseits ist der Wagen (^{GIŠ}MAR.GÍD.DA) mit Stiergespann im Textfragment KUB 28.5 (+) VBoT 73 Rs. III 3' (Dupl. KUB 28.4 Rs. 2') belegt, das zu CTH 727 gehört und Attribute eines Wettergottes hattischer Herkunft beschreibt[12]. Alle unter CTH 727 gebuchten Textfragmente sind jüngeren Datums, aber eine bruchstückhaftige Darstellung des Wettergottes mit seiner Karre auf einer Scherbe der Reliefvase weist auf die Anwesenheit dieser Vorstellung bereits in der anatolischen Kunst althethitischer Zeit[13]. KBo 17.85 kann sich also auf einen vorhurritischen Wettergott beziehen, was um so mehr wahrscheinlich ist, als in diesem Text die Sänger in hattischer Sprache singen. Folglich gehört der Wettergot und sein Wagen mit Stiergespann sowohl zur hattischen als auch zur hurritischen Überlieferung, und diese überraschende Ähnlichkeit der Vorstellungen der Wettergötter verschiedener Herkunft bedarf einer Erklärung.

^{GIŠ}TUKUL gehört zur Ausrüstung des Teššub im Textfragment KBo 23.47 (Rs. III 4') mit Duplikat 125/r[14], doch ist diese Waffe hier nur zusätzlich er-

---

[11] Wegen der Nennung der Berge (ḪUR.SAG^{MEŠ}, IV 9'), die auch in der Aufzählung der Attribute des Teššub VS N.F. XII Nr. 2 belegt sind (I 9).

[12] Zu dieser Textgruppe s. A. Kammenhuber, *Die protohattisch-hethitische Bilinguis vom Mond, der vom Himmel gefallen ist*, ZA 51 (1955) 102-123.

[13] Vgl. K. Bittel, *Fragment einer hethitischen Reliefvase von Boğazköy*, in A. Kuschke-E. Kutsch (Hg.), *Archäologie und Altes Testament, Festschrift für Kurt Galling* (1970) 19ff.; R. M. Boehmer, *Die Reliefkeramik von Boğazköy* (Berlin 1983) 36ff.

[14] Zu diesem Text s. H. G. Güterbock in H. Otten et al. (Hg.), *Hittite and Other Anatolian and Near Eastern Studies in Honour of Sedat Alp* (Ankara 1992) 238f.

wähnt, und am Anfang der Aufzählung taucht ein Speer (^{GIŠ}ŠUKUR) als seine Hauptwaffe auf. Der Speer erscheint ebenfalls anstatt der Keule unter den Attributen des „mächtigen Wettergottes" (^{D}U NIR.GÁL) in KUB 20.65, 10' (CTH 670). Dem Text ist zu entnehmen, daß wir es hier mit einer Kultgestalt des Teššub zu tun haben, und dieser Schluß wird durch andere Ritualtexte der hurritischen Schicht bestätigt, in denen dieser Gott auftritt[15]. Der „mächtige Wettergott" spielt in den Annalen Muršilis II eine große Rolle. Dies läßt vielleicht erklären, warum er insbesondere in Katapa verehrt wurde[16]: wie bekannt, war Katapa eine Lieblingsstadt dieses Königs und seine Winterresidenz. Es bleibt noch zu bemerken, daß in der anatolischen Kunst der Speer vor allem als Waffe des Schutzgottes auftaucht.

Im Lichte sowohl der Bildkunst als auch der oben angeführten Textfragmente scheint es möglich zu sein, daß der Teššub von Ḫalab auf seinem Weg nach Anatolien sein vielleicht wichtigstes Attribut, d.h. seine siegreichen Waffen, verloren hat. Erwähnenswert ist dabei, daß im 14.-13. Jahrhundert v. Chr. auch der ugaritische Wettergott ohne beide Keulen dargestellt wird, die ihm der Mythos zuschreibt. Trotzdem lassen sich in den Boğazköy-Texten einige Spuren älterer Überlieferung finden. Vor allem ist hier ein kleines, schlecht erhaltenes Textfragment KBo 39.90 zu nennen (s. oben).

Im hurritischen Kultkreis ist das hurritische, seit mittelhethitischer Zeit bezeugte Wort *šauri* „Waffen"[17] gewöhnlich mit der Göttin Šauška gebunden, aber gelegentlich sind auch *šauri* des Teššub belegt; vgl. KUB 34.102 Vs. II 25f. mit seinem Duplikat KUB 32.84 Rs. IV 5'f.

Diese spärlichen Dokumente weisen daraufhin, daß die Vorstellung der siegreichen Waffen des Teššub in gewissem Grade auch in Kleinasien bekannt wurde und daß die Waffen selbst in mindestens einem Tempel dieses Gottes als Kultobjekt verehrt wurde. Es sei noch daran erinnert, daß im Hethitischen das Adjektiv *tarḫuili-* „siegreich" als Attribut zu ^{GIŠ}ŠUKUR bzw. zu *turi-* „Speer" vorkommt[18], wobei sich jene Waffe in diesem Fall auf keinen Gott bezieht. Als Attribut zu ^{GIŠ}TUKUL wurde gelegentlich das Adj. NIR.GÁL-*i-*/**muwattalli-* „stark, mächtig" verwendet; vgl. den Ausdruck ^{GIŠ}TUKUL($^{\text{ḪI.A}}$) NIR.GÁL(-*i*-) in KBo 2.32 Rs. 3, KBo 11.28 Vs. II 8', KUB 44.33 Vs. II 5', VS N.F. XII Nr. 7 Rs. IV 17 und Nr. 26 Rs. 15'.

---

[15] Vgl. KUB 20.27, 3' und KUB 44.47 Vs. I 9', II 3', 9', 12', Rs.V x+1 (erg.), VI 7' (Kultzeremonie in ^{É}*arkiu*), überdies KUB 25.41 Rs. V 13'f. und KUB 10.20, 5'.

[16] Zum Kult dieses Gottes in Katapa s. KUB 9.16 Vs. I 8ff. (dritter Tag des *nuntarrijašḫaš*-Festes), KUB 25.10 (dem Kolophon nach das Herbstfest für diesen Gott in Katapa).

[17] Vgl. KBo 32.209, 8' (Fragment der hurritisch-hethitischen Bilingue) und s. dazu E. Neu, *Das hurritische Epos der Freilassung* I (Wiesbaden 1996 = StBoT 32) 547.

[18] S. dazu E. Neu, *Der Anitta-Text* (Wiesbaden 1974 = StBoT 18) 29.

A NEOLITHIC FEMALE REVEALING HER BREASTS*

Denise Schmandt-Besserat
Professor of Art
The University of Texas at Austin

The paper deals with a Neolithic statue depicting a woman holding her breasts (fig. 1 a and b). The figure was excavated at ‘Ain Ghazal, near Amman, Jordan, a site first settled about 7250 B.C., in the so-called Pre-Pottery Neolithic B period (PPNB). In a matter of a few centuries the village of stone houses had spread over 30 acres along the Zarqa River, making it one of the largest known Neolithic settlements in the Near East.[1] During a prosperous period of farming ca. 7250-6000 B.C., ‘Ain Ghazal witnessed what could be termed an explosion of symbolism. The community created an array of new symbols. Symbols are understood here as things loaded with significance that allow us to conceive ideas, communicate them and share them with others (for example, the cross or flags are common symbols in our own society). The PPNB symbolic assemblage of ‘Ain Ghazal included human and animal figurines,[2] tokens of many shapes,[3] motifs painted on house floors, modeled human skulls and statues. The figure discussed in this paper, is part of the latter genre. Although the statue is prehistoric it is of interest to Sumerologists because the gesture of a female clutching her breasts is also typical of later icons interpreted as representations of Inanna. It is with great pleasure that I dedicate this paper to Krystyna Szarzyńska who contributed towards our understanding of the Sumerian goddess.

---

* I am grateful to G. O. Rollefson and Zeidan Kafafi, co-directors of the ‘Ain Ghazal excavations, for the great privilege of working on the symbolic material of the site. I also thank Pierre Bikai, Director, The American Center of Oriental Research, Amman, for discussing the paper with me and for his most helpful suggestions. The study was funded by a Fellowship from the American Center of Oriental Research, Amman, Jordan and a grant from the Near and Middle East Research and Training Program.

[1] G. O. Rollefson, A. H. Simmons and Z. Kafafi, *Neolithic Cultures at ‘Ain Ghazal, Jordan,* Journal of Field Archaeology, Vol. 19, No. 4, 1992, p. 444.

[2] D. Schmandt-Besserat, *Animal Symbols at ‘Ain Ghazal*, Expedition, Vol. 39, No. 1, 1997.

[3] D. Schmandt-Besserat, *Before Writing* (Austin 1992) vol. 1, p. 32; vol. 2, p.405-406; H. Iceland, *Token Finds at Pre-Pottery ‘Ain Ghazal, Jordan: A Formal and Technical Analysis*, forthcoming.

The 'Ain Ghazal collection of 31 statues, some about 1 meter tall, is unique and most impressive. No other 8-7th millennium Neolithic site in the Near East has produced such an array of „monumental" figures. The statues were discovered in two separate caches, beneath the floors of long abandoned houses, outside the inhabited area. The female holding her breasts belongs to Cache 1 found in 1983 and dated to ca. 6750 +/- 80 B.C.[4] It was part of a group of 25 statues, including 13 full figures and 12 busts, carefully laid in tiers in a pit visibly dug for the sole purpose of disposing of the icons.[5] Cache 2, excavated in 1985,[6] held six statues [7] of a date estimated to ca. 6500 B.C.

The female presented here shares all the basic characteristics of the two sets of statues. Like the other figures, it was made of plaster. The manufacture involved building a core of reed bundles tightly bound with twine, then applying and modeling a thick layer of fresh plaster.

The statue is one of the smallest examples of the two sets of figures.[8] However, compared to the previous Mesolithic or the contemporaneous Neolithic minuscule human clay figurines, the 80 cm high piece may be termed monumental. The figure is about 10-15 cm thick in section. In other words, it is flat, almost two-dimensional. The back is straight except for slightly projecting buttocks. The icon is well-balanced in order to stand.

The head is emphasized, representing about one-sixth of the total size of the statue. Above the forehead, a recessed feature shows traces of black paint or bitumen, whereas the face is treated with ochre and given a silky finish. This peculiar ridge is usually interpreted as having probably held a headdress or a wig of a different material.[9] The neck is oversized. The stylization involves manipulating the proportions of the human face. The high forehead is almost half the size of the head. The eyes are low compared to the brows and nose, and so are the cheek bones. The brows, nose, labial canal and mouth are arranged in a T-shape. The lug-shaped ears are high and close to the eyes. The facial features are striking. The nose is conspicuously short and upturned, exhibiting long, thin nostrils. The minuscule mouth has no lips. The chin is round. The woman has a stern expression and arresting glance. The eyes are

---

[4] G. O. Rollefson and A. H. Simmons, *The Early Neolithic Village of 'Ain Ghazal, Jordan: Preliminary Report on the 1983 Season*, BASOR Supplement No 23, 1985, p. 48-50.

[5] K. Walker Tubb, and C. A. Grissom, *'Ayn Ghazal: A Comparative Study of the 1983 and 1985 Statuary Caches*, Studies in the History and Archaeology of Jordan, Vol. V (Amman 1995) p. 437-447.

[6] G. O. Rollefson and A. H. Simmons, *The Neolithic Village of Ain Ghazal, Jordan: Preliminary Report on the 1985 Season*, BASOR Supplement No 25, 1987, p. 95-96.

[7] C. A. Grissom, *Conservation of Neolithic Lime Plaster Statues from Áin Ghazal*, in A. Roy and P. Smith (eds.), *Archaeological Conservation and Its Consequences*, (London 1996). p. 70-75.

[8] Op. cit., p. 72.

[9] A. Gunther, *Preserving Ancient Statues From Jordan*, in Arthur M. Sackler Gallery, Smithsonian Institution, 1996-97.

disproportionately large – twice the size of the nose and many times that of the mouth. They are set far below the brows and far apart. The oval eyeballs bulge slightly, surrounded by a deep, oval ridge filled with black bitumen. The cornea is painted with a black iris. The eyelids are not portrayed.

The body is carefully modeled. The shoulders slope gently. The two breasts are placed low on the chest. They hang tightly parallel, ending with no nipples. The waist is clearly marked and the pelvis and buttocks are sensitively rendered, including a light bulge suggesting fatty thighs. The genitalia are omitted. The legs are naturalistically rendered. Feet are poorly preserved on the statues of Cache 1. The fragments available indicate that the figures originally had short and wide feet with toes, sometimes numbering 6, were cut with slashes of inconsistent lengths extending through half of the feet. The toenails, however, were carefully pictured. The female statue was treated with ochre before being smoothed but does not show any painting, whereas others from Cache 1 display red lines around the shoulders and along the thighs and legs seemingly depicting bodices and pants.

Most of the 'Ain Ghazal statues are shown with a flat chest and no arms. Our female is exceptional in emphatically exhibiting two clearly modeled breasts. She folds disproportionately small arms, devoid of forearms, to reach the chest. She stretches her hands in a fan-shape to frame the bosom. The movement is awkwardly rendered. The arms are skimpy, the fingers are cut sloppily and their number seems not to matter since the right hand is designed with seven. However, the woman revealing her breast while staring sternly at the viewer makes a potent statement.

The female is not unique in executing the striking gesture. It is repeated by two other statues from 'Ain Ghazal, also from Cache 1. In the first, the head and entire left side is destroyed, but a small hand is clearly visible at the chest.[10] In the second, the schematic treatment of the limbs and chest compromise the effect. The figure curves her arms across the torso, but the limbs are reduced to thin, crescent-shaped stumps that fail to reach the breast; there are no fingers pointing to the bosom, and finally; the breasts are small and thin resembling animal udders. Although the message was probably meant to be the same in the two figures, the first is explicit, while the second remains ambiguous.

The 'Ain Ghazal statues may not be the earliest examples of the eye-catching symbol. This distinction may be deserved by a small Jericho clay

[10] G. O. Rollefson and A. H. Simmons, *The Early Neolithic Village of 'Ain Ghazal, Jordan: Preliminary Report on the 1983 Season*, BASOR Supplement No 23, 1985, p. 50, fig. 13; G. O. Rollefson, *Ritual and Ceremony at Neolithic Ain Ghazal, (Jordan)*, JFA, Vol. 9, No. 2, 1983, p. 31, Pl. I: 1.

figurine of a woman holding her breasts, found by Kenyon in a PPNB shrine.[11] The Jericho example is precious in that it shows that the motif was already popular in the PPNB. After the Neolithic period, the gesture was to enjoy a lifetime of some five millennia in Near Eastern iconography (fig. 2). It is repeated from the Mediterranean Sea[12] to the Zagros Mountains[13] in innumerable figures until the first millennium B.C.[14] The gesture of a female revealing her breasts is generally interpreted as a symbol of nurturing and fertility. It is regarded as the hallmark of Near Eastern goddesses.[15] The figurines could conceivably represent An's consort, the goddess An/Antum whose breasts were deemed to be the source of the rain beneficent for vegetation.[16] However, the images of females holding their breasts are generally viewed as personifying the goddess of love and fertility revered through the ages under the names of Inanna, Ishtar, Asherath, Astarte or Tanit. This tradition is supported by hymns preserved in cuneiform texts. Some praise Ishtar as "... the mother of the faithful breast..." or the goddess ..." nourishing humanity on her breast..."[17] Particularly telling is also the following prayer of a king to Inanna to give him her breast, from which he will drink as a symbol of the fertility of the land.

„Oh lady, your breast is your field,
Inanna, your breast is your field,
Your wide field which 'pours out' plants,
Your wide field which 'pours out' grain,
Water flowing from on high-(for) the lord-bread
from on high,
Water flowing, flowing from on high-(for) the lord-
bread, bread from on high,
[Pour]out for the 'commanded' lord,
I will drink it from you."[18]

---

[11] K. M. Kenyon, *Digging up Jericho* (New York 1957) p. 85.

[12] L. Badre, *The Terra Cotta Anthropomorphic Figurines*, Studies in the History and Archaeology of Jordan, Vol. V (Amman 1995) p. 459: a, b; 460: a, c, d, e, g; 461: a-d; 463: c; 466: a, b, g, h.; V. Karageorghis, *The Civilization of Prehistoric Cyprus*, (Athens 1976) fig. 103.

[13] A. Spycket, *Les Figurines de Suse*, Mémoires de la Délégation Archéologique en Iran, Vol. 52, 1992.

[14] L. Badre, *Les Figurines Anthropomorphes en Terre Cuite à l'Age du Bronze en Syrie*, (Paris 1980). p. 387: 32, Pl. LX: 32.

[15] L. Badre, *The Terra Cotta Anthropomorphic Figurines*, Studies in the History and Archaeology of Jordan, Vol. V (Amman 1995) p. 465.

[16] T. Jacobsen, *The Treasures of Darkness* (New Haven 1976) p. 95.

[17] S. Langdon, *Tammuz and Ishtar* (Oxford 1914) p. 60 and 64.

[18] S. N. Kramer, *Dumuzi and Inanna: Prayer for Water and Bread*, in ANET, p. 641-642.

In sum, from the Neolithic to the Babylonian period, the figures of women exhibiting their breasts were metaphors. They used the every day life experience of a tender mother nursing her child to express the bounty of nature. The 'Ain Ghazal statue, and the Jericho figurine, are testimonies to the everlasting endurance of symbolism. The icons showing females clutching their breasts provide the evidence that the forceful image of a goddess nursing mankind had its root in the Neolithic, as early as 6500 B.C. In fact, the symbol may be viewed as a creation typical of the beginning of agriculture. There is little doubt that fertility acquired a new pressing significance when the survival of sedentary populations depended on the production of fields and orchards. It is therefore to be expected that new deities emerged in the farmers pantheon, followed by new rituals that were deemed to insure bountiful harvests and prosperous flocks. The gesture of the female exhibiting her breasts was a potent symbol fostering a new ideology[19] that eventually paved the way for the cult of Inanna.

[19] O. Bar-Yosef and R. H. Meadow, *The Origin of Agriculture in the Near East*, in T. Douglas Price and A. Birgette Gebauer (eds.), *Last Hunters, First Farmers: New Perspectives on the Prehistoric Transition to Agriculture*, (Santa Fe 1995) p. 80.

ILLUSTRATIONS

Figure 1 a and b. Statue of a woman revealing her breast, 'Ain Ghazal, Cache 1. Photo by Hussein Debajah, courtesy The Institute of Archaeology and Anthropology, Yarmouk University, Irbid, Jordan.

Figure 2. Females presenting their breasts, designed by Lamia Salem el-Khoury.

a. Hacilar VI type, cream and burnished statuette, James Mellaart, *Excavations at Hacilar*, Vol. 2 (Edinburg 1970) p. 233, pl. CLXXVI.

b. Tell Mardikh, after L. Badre, *The Terra Cotta Anthropomorphic Figurines*, in Studies in the History and Archaeology of Jordan, Vol. V (Amman 1995) p. 460, fig. 2: c.

c. Tell Chuera, after L. Badre, *The Terra Cotta Anthropomorphic Figurines*, in Studies in the History and Archaeology of Jordan, Vol. V (Amman 1995) p. 463, fig. 4: c.

d. Alalakh, after L. Badre, *The Terra Cotta Anthropomorphic Figurines*, in Studies in the History and Archaeology of Jordan, Vol. V (Amman 1995) p. 466, fig. 6: a.

e. Kamid al-Lawz, After L. Badre, *The Terra Cotta Anthropomorphic Figurines*, in Studies in the History and Archaeology of Jordan, Vol. V (Amman 1995) p. 466, fig. 6: h.

May 19, 1997

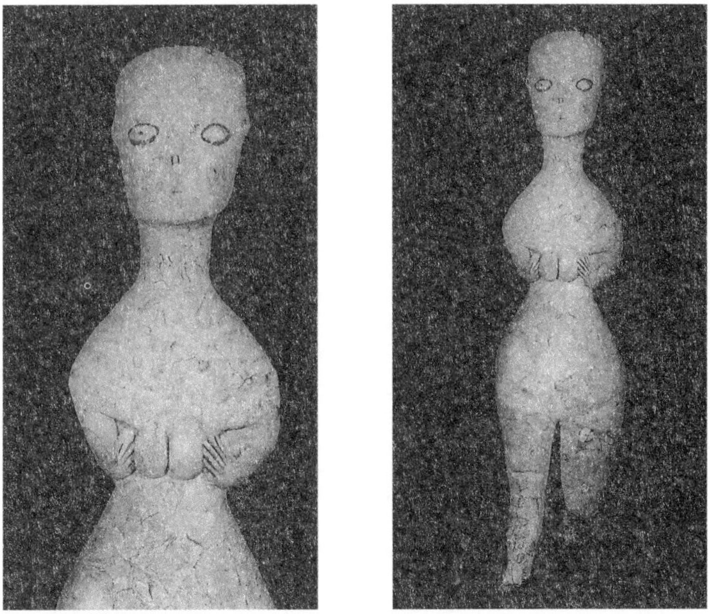

Fig. 1

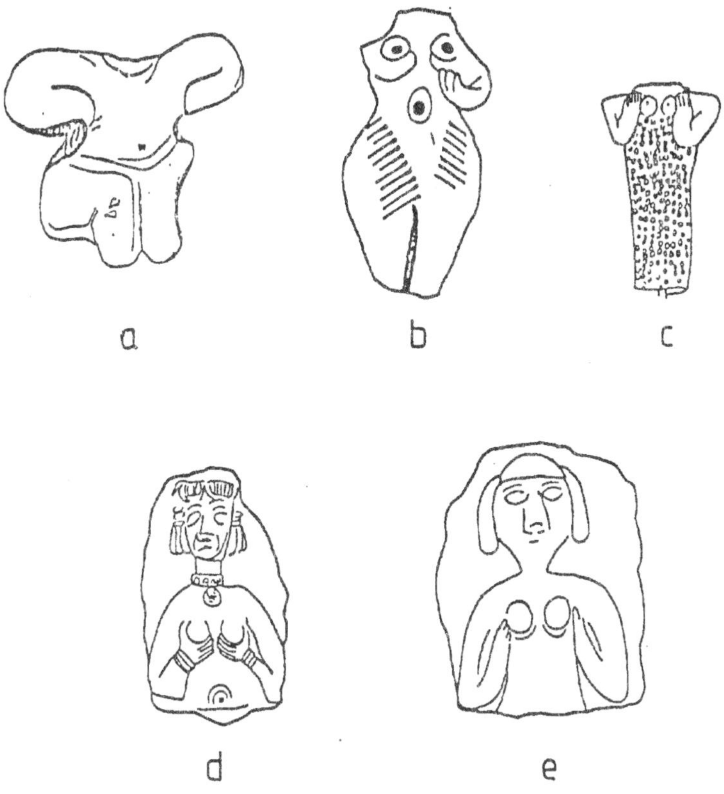

Fig. 2

INANNA'S ARCHAIC SYMBOL

Piotr Steinkeller
Harvard University

1. It is a true pleasure to be able to include this little piece in the volume honoring Dr. Krystyna Szarzyńska, whose steadfast and loving preoccupation with the archaic texts from Uruk has contributed so much toward a keener understanding of the earliest stages of the cuneiform. My satisfaction is still greater that the present paper touches on two of our Honoree's favorite topics: the archaic divine emblems*[1] and the goddess Inanna.[2]

2. Of all the items belonging to the visual repertoire of archaic Uruk art, none is more common and characteristic than the volute-like reed structure. This object, consisting of a pole topped with a ring and streamers, is depicted, often in pairs, either free-standing or mounted on altars and the roofs of sheep- and cattle-pens (figs. 1, 2 and 3). There also survive clay models of this object (figs. 4, 5 and 6), which appear to have been parts of friezes decorating the walls of temples.[3] Because of its formal identity with the archaic sign MÙŠ/INANNA (= ZATU-374, 375), the volute-like structure can confidently be identified as a symbol of Inanna.[4] Since no certain depictions of it are extant from later periods,[5] the active life of this symbol in cult apparently did not

---

* Abbreviations are those of the *Chicago Assyrian Dictionary* and the *Philadelphia Sumerian Dictionary*.

[1] *Some of the Oldest Cult Symbols in Archaic Uruk*, JEOL 30 (1987-88) 3-21; *Some Comments on Individual Entries in the Uruk Sign-List* ZATU, ASJ 18 (1996) 235-238; *Archaic Sumerian Standards*, JCS 48 (1996) (in press).

[2] *The Sumerian Goddess* INANA-KUR, Orientalia Varsoviensia 1 (1987) 7-14; *Kult bogini Inany w Uruk w okresie archaicznym*, Euhemer - Przegląd Religioznawczy 1988/2, pp. 3-11; *Offerings for the Goddess Inana in Archaic Uruk*, RA 87 (1993) 7-26.

[3] See J. Jordan, UVB 2 (1931), pp. 33-36; E. Heinrich, *Bauwerke in der altsumerischen Bildkunst*, Schriften der Max Freiherr von Oppenheim-Stiftung, Heft 2 (Wiesbaden 1957), pp. 31-32.

[4] See already A. Falkenstein, ATU 1, p. 59.

[5] See P. Amiet, *La glyptique mésopotamienne archaïque*, 2nd ed. (Paris 1980), p. 79. J. Black and A. Green, *Gods, Demons and Symbols of Ancient Mesopotamia* (Austin 1992), p. 154, claim that „after the Uruk period, the symbol is to be found, though rarely, until the Early Dynastic Period," but I am unaware of any such evidence.

extend beyond Uruk times. It did, however, survive till the very end of cuneiform civilization, as the traditional graph of Inanna's name.

The volute-like symbol of Inanna is one of several reed emblems that are represented in Uruk art.[6] Two more of those can be identified with certainty: (1) a pole with a triangle, the so-called „buckled post" or „Bügelschaft", which is identical with the sign ŠEŠ/NANNA$_X$ (= ZATU-595), a symbol of Nanna[7]; and (2) a pole with pairs of rings, the so-called „ringed-pole", which is identical with the sign NUN (ZATU-421), a symbol of Enki.[8] We can be certain that the Sumerian word describing such emblems was urin(URI$_3$), a well-documented designation of divine emblems in later periods.[9] This identification is assured by the fact that URI$_3$ (= ZATU-523) is a close relative of ŠEŠ/NANNA$_X$. It would appear, therefore, that URI$_3$ was derived from ŠEŠ/NANNA$_X$ to serve as a generic designation of such emblems.

As is indicated equally by the visual and epigraphic data, the urin emblems were large, usually free-standing effigies, made of reeds or wood,[10] which were permanently (or at least semi-permanently) erected at cultic sites. These characteristics (which make them comparable to totem poles[11]) set the urin apart from the other type of divine emblems known from ancient Mesopota-

---

6 See Szarzyńska, *Cult Symbols*.

7 See ibid, pp. 6-7, 12-13; Steinkeller, BiOr 52 (1995) 705, 709.

8 It appears likely that this symbol represents a tree. Note that in *Enki and the World Order* 166-167 (cited below p. 91) the urin of Enki set-up in the Abzu is said to be a shade-giving umbrella. It is significant that, elswhere in the same composition, Enki is likened to a shady mes-tree planted in the Abzu: lugal ^{giš}mes Abzu-ta/-a dù-a kur-ra íl-la ušum[gal] ma, Eridug^{ki}-ga gub-ba [gis]su-bi an ki-a dul-la $^{\text{[giš]}}$tir (giš) gurun-na kalam-ma lá-a, „the master (Enki) is a mes-tree planted in the Abzu; it towers over the lands; it is a huge dragon standing in Eridu; its shade covers heaven and earth; it is (like) a forest of fruit (bearing) trees stretching over the country" (*Enki and the World Order* 4-7). A similar image of Enki is found in MDP 14, p. 125 lines 2-13 (a Srgonic incantation), where he is compared to a shady *kiškanû*-tree growing in the „pure place" (i.e., Abzu): [lugal] giš-kín-gim [ki-si]kil mú-a ^{d}En-ki giš-kín-gim ki-sikil mú-a kur-ku-rá-a-ni kur hé-gál sug$_4$ ki DU.DU-ni gissu-bi suh za:gìn-na-gim ab-šag$_4$-ga lá-a lugal giš-kín-gim ki-sikil-e íb-mú-a-gim ^{d}En-ki giš-kín-gim [ki-siki]l-e íb-mú-a-gim, „[the master] grew up in a pure place like a *kiškanû*-tree; Enki grew up in a pure place like a *kiškanû*-tree; his flood-waves fill the land(s) with abundance; the shade of his 'place of standing' stretches into the midst of the sea like a lapis diadem; the master is like a *kiškanû*-tree that the pure place made grow; Enki is like a *kiškanû*-tree that the pure place made grow".

9 Corresponding to Akk. *urinnu*. Also urin-gal, Akk. *urigallu*/**uringallu*. See B. Pongratz-Leisten, BaghMitt 23 (1992) 306-308, 318-330; AHw., pp. 1429-1430.

10 According to Gudea Cyl. A xxii 20 (cited below p. 91), a wooden Shar'ur effigy was set up as a „large emblem" (urin-gal). The fashioning of such wooden effiges is described in detail elsewhere in the Gudea corpus: $^{\text{(mušen)}}$šár-ùr (Statue B v 28-38, vi 45-50; Cyl. A xv 22-25); šár-gaz (Statue B v 39-40).

11 For this suggestion, see already Falkenstein in *The Near East: The Early Civilizations*, Delacorte World History vol. 2, J. Bottéro et al. (eds.), (New York 1967), p. 47: „The most frequent symbols we see are polelike objects: the 'gateposts' or 'reed-bundles' of Inanna of Uruk and the 'buckled post' of Nanna the moon-god of Ur are the best-known. Totems? It is possible."

mia, the šu-nir.[12] The latter object, to be identified as „standard," consisted of a pole with a tasseled cross-bar, on which there was mounted a divine symbol.[13] Unlike the urin, the šu-nir were portable.[14] The difference between the two types of objects[15] is best demonstrated by the following passage, in which a šu-nir standard is substituted for / applied as an urin emblem: ka-al nam-nun-na mi-ni-gar-ra-ni IM-dugud$_{x}$(MI)^{mušen} šu-nir lugal-la-na-kam urin-šè bí-mul, „at the clay pit, which he had set up in princely splendor, he displayed / made glitter as a divine emblem the Thunderbird, the standard of his master" (Gudea Cyl. A xiii 21-23). The šu-nir were known already in Uruk times, as is proved by the surviving representations of such standards.[16]

3. While it is certain that the volute-like structure represents a symbol of Inanna, its meaning remains a mystery. The fact that this object is occasionally shown in connection with sheep- and cattle-pens led W. Andrae to interpret it as a doorpost of the primitive reed hut.[17] As envisioned by Andrae, a pair of such doorposts supported in their volutes a cross-bar, over which there was rolled a reed mat functioning as a door-covering.[18] However, an examination of the scenes in question shows clearly that, rather than constituting an organic part of the pen, the volute-like structure is but a decorative appendage, which

12 Corresponding to Akk. *šurinnu*. See, most recently, Pongratz-Leisten, op. cit., pp. 302-306, 308-318; J. Spaey, „Emblems in Rituals in the Old Babylonian Period," in J. Quaegebeur (ed.), *Ritual and Sacrifice in the Ancient Near East*, OLA 55 (Leuven 1993), pp. 411-420; CAD Š/3, pp. 344-347.

13 Depictions of individuals carrying such standards are found on the fragments of Gudea stelae (G. Cros, NFT, p. 29), which can be correlated with Gudea Cyl. A xiv 7-27 (for which see the following note).

14 Among the 3rd mil. evidence, note that šu-nir standards were carried by the territorial clans (im-ru-a) of Ningirsu, Inanna, and Nanshe as they were mobilized to build the Eninnu (Gudea Cyl. A xiv 7-27). The šu-nir were also used in battle, as shown by the Pre-Sargonic royal inscriptions from Lagash (for attestations, see H. Steible, FAOS 6, p. 61).

15 Rather surprisingly, Pongratz-Leisten, op. cit., p. 303, thinks that the data extant „lassen eine Differenzierung in dem Gebrauch der beide Begriffe šu.nir und urì nicht zu."

16 See Amiet, *Glyptique*, pl. 46 no. 658.

17 W. Andrae, *Das Gotteshaus und die Urformen des Bauens im Alten Orient* (Berlin 1930) (especially pp. 48-50, 56); *Die Ionische Säule: Bauform oder Symbol?* (Berlin 1933). This hypothesis had a broad following at one time, and it is still accepted by some scholars. See, e.g., H. Frankfort, *Cylinder Seals* (London 1939), p. 15 („gatepost with streamer"); E. D. Van Buren, AfO 13 (1939-41) 33, 39-40 („gatepost with streamers"); E. Williams-Forte in D. Wolkstein and S. N. Kramer, *Inanna: Queen of Heaven and Earth* (New York 1983), p. 188 („gatepost emblems of Inanna"); Black and Green, *Gods*, p. 154 („a doorpost for a structure built of reeds and probably made of a bundle of reeds bound together, with the upper ends bent over to make a loop for the crosspole").

18 Ibid., p. 56 and fig. 48a.

is attached to the pen's roof.[19] A corroboration of this is provided by the parallel images of the volute-like structure being mounted on altars, which prove that it is an independent, architecturally unrelated object.

But, beyond Andrae's suggestion, no one has ever attempted to assign to the volute-like structure any specific meaning. The prevailing opinion is that the symbol is devoid of any representational content.[20] Thus, scholars have been content to refer to it purely descriptively, by using such designations as „*Schilfringbündel*"[21] „a shaft with a banner,"[22] „la hampe à banderole,"[23] „ring-headed post, usually with streamers,"[24] or „'roller-blind' reed pylon."[25]

A possible light on this problem is thrown by an ED literary passage, which, if our interpretation is correct, identifies the volute-like symbol of Inanna as a specific object. The passage in question comes from a composition concerning Ama'ushum(galana),[26] of which three mss. survive, stemming from Ebla (two) and Abu Salabikh (one) respectively:

ARET 5 20 + A. Archi, QS 18 (1992) 36-37 (pls. 7-8) = Source A.

ARET 5 21 + Archi, Or. NS 58 (1989) 125 + QS 18, pp. 38-39 (pls. 9-10) = Source B.

OIP 99 278 = Source C.

(1)

A vii 7: za-gir bar-su gú ^{d}Inanna lá-lá
B viii 5: za-gir bar-su gú ^{d}Inanna lá-lá
C iii 1-2: za-gìn bar-⌈sikil⌉ gú ^{d}Inanna lá

„the lapis lazuli / lustrous … binding the neck of Inanna,"

(2)
A viii 1: urin-gal-gal é ^{d}⌈Inanna⌉-dar an-si-ga
B viii 6: [...]⌈é⌉ ^{d}⌈Inanna⌉-dar an-si-ga

19 For a thorough critique of Andrae's theory, see Amiet, *Glyptique*, pp. 80-82. See also E. Heinrich, *Bauwerke*, pp. 31-38.

20 So, e.g., U. Seidl, RLA 3 (1969) 490, who classifies it as „anikonisch".

21 E.g., Seidl, op. cit., p. 490.

22 P. P. Delougaz, JNES 27 (1968) 196.

23 Amiet, *Glyptique*, p. 78.

24 Black and Green, *Gods*, p. 154.

25 T. Jacobsen, Aula Orientalis 9 (1991) 117 n. 22.

26 A complete edition of this composition is foreseen by D. R. Frayne.

C iii 3: urin-gal-gal Kul-ab$_4$-da si-ga

„the great urin emblems set up (lit.: driven in) at the temple of Inanna / at Kulaba,"

(3)
A viii 2: za-i gal-gal Gul-la-ab-dar si-ga
B viii 7: za-i gal-[ga]l Gul-[l]a-[...]
C: omits

„the great spires set up (lit.: driven in) at Kulaba."

I submit that these three lines form a single unit, with lines (2) and (3) standing in apposition to line (1). At the very least, it is certain that (2) is in apposition to (3). The meaning of (2) is clear. The construction urin-gal-ø X-da si-(g), „to embed / set up[27] a great emblem in X," is found also in Gudea inscriptions: ^{giš}šár-ùr-bi urin-gal-gim Lagaš^{ki}-da im-da-si, „he set up in Lagash a wooden Shar'ur (effigy) as a great emblem" (Cyl. A xxii 20); urin-gal Lagaš^{ki}-da si-ga-bi, „its great emblems, set up in Lagash" (Cyl. B xxii 5). Notice further its occurrence in *Enki and the World Order* 166-167: urin-gal Abzu-ta si-ga an-dùl-le-eš ak-a gissu-bi ki-šár-ra lá-a ùku-e ní-[t]e-en-te, „the great emblem (of Enki) set up / embedded in the Abzu, made into a protecting umbrella, its shade stretches to the horizon, the people revive themselves (under it)".

In view of the parallelism between (2) and (3), one may a priori conclude that the item za-i, appearing in (3), was an object somehow similar to the urin emblem. Without any doubt, the word hiding behind za-i is the well-known architectural term zà-è. The latter word denotes a type of protruding element, which, as the extant attestations show, could be found on the top of public buildings (such as temples or palaces) or fortification walls.[28] This evidence indicates that zà-è should be identified as „spire," „pinnacle," or „finial."[29] As such, therefore, it was not unlike the urin.

---

[27] For this sense of si-(g), see the examples collected by S. Dunham, RA 80 (1986) 40-45, in which si-(g) denotes the setting up (or the placing in) of various post-like objects.

[28] For zà-è, which is equated with *zamû ša* BÀD, *sippu*, and *āṣītu*, see Å. Sjöberg, TCS 3, pp. 57-58; C. Wilcke, *Lugalbanda*, p. 221; J. Klein, TAPS 71/7 (Philadelphia 1981), p. 39. Among its occurrences, note especially *Temple Hymns* 31 and *Nungal Hymn* 17, where zà-è is said to be part of the dub-lá, „portico" or „pilaster", for which see, most recently, A. R. George, *Iraq* 57 (1995) 185-186.

[29] For this conclusion, see already Wilcke, op. cit., p. 221: „[zà-è] einen herausragenden Teil der Mauer bezeichnen: Zinnen oder Mauertürme." Here notice that this term occurs already in a Pre-Sargonic (or Early Sargonic) tablet from Nippur, which records roofbeams (giš-ùr) that came „from the battlements (of the temple?) of Ishkur": zà-è ^{d}Iškur-ta (Westenholz Jena 217:6).

If I am correct that lines (2) and (3) stand in apposition to line (1), it follows then that the „great emblems of Inanna", further described as „great spires", are qualifications of the lapis lazuli object which, according to (1), „binds the neck of Inanna". Assuming, as it seems very likely, that the urin-gal of Inanna mentioned in our passage are identical with Inanna's symbol of Uruk art, we could find here an explanation as to what this symbol actually depicts or, to be more precise, as to what it was *thought* to depict in Early Dynastic times, when the composition in question presumably was written down. This caveat is necessary, since, as noted earlier, there is unfortunately no proof that the symbol continued to be used in cult after the Uruk period (though it survived under the guise of the sign MÙŠ, whose symbolic connection with Inanna has undoubtedly continued to be generally recognized).

We need, therefore, to consider the meaning of that mysterious lapis lazuli object, whose name is alternatively written bar-su and bar-sikil. In my opinion, the only way in which these variant spellings can be harmonized and made to agree with the information that the object in question „binds the neck of Inanna" (meaning, accordingly, that one finds here either a jewelry item or a piece of feminine apparel) is to analyze bar-su and bar-sikil as graphic variants[30] of the word usually spelled bar-si, bar-si-ig, or bar-sig (Akk. *paršikku*), denoting a type of scarf or shawl.[31]

This piece of apparel was made of linen or wool, and could be worn over the neck or head, or even over the hands.[32] Although there survive mentions of the bar-si made for kings,[33] this appears to have been a typically feminine article. Of special interest here is the fact that the bar-si are included in the inventories of garments and jewelry belonging to Annunitum[34] and Ishtar of Lagaba,[35] both of whom, of course, were but variant forms of Inanna. This evidence demonstrates that the bar-si was a standard element of the garb donned by the statues of Inanna/Ishtar. In this connection, one should also note the existence, in Pre-Sargonic Lagash, of a headgear called men bar-su, which is documented for (the statues of) Inanna[36] and Nanshe.[37] It appears quite likely

---

[30] To be precise: bar-sug$_6$(SU) and bar-sik(il) respectively.

[31] See PSD B, pp. 126-127 („sash, shawl"): AHw., p. 836 („Kopfbinde, Mitze"); W. F. Leemans, *Ishtar of Lagaba and Her Dress*, SLB I/1 (Leiden 1952), pp. 12-13 („a ribbon or a shawl"). Cf. also bar-siki, listed in PSD B, p. 128, which may be yet another spelling of this word.

[32] See PSD B, pp. 126-127.

[33] See ibid., p. 126.

[34] 2 ^{túg}bar-si zi-li-hi (MVN 33 152:3).

[35] Leemans, op. cit., p. 1-2, lines 16-17, 32-33, listing eighteen bar-si of two different types.

[36] 1 men-bar-su ^{d}Inanna Ib-gal (BIN 8 390 i 3-4).

that the object in question was a crown with an attached scarf or band,[38] which either was rolled around the crown's top or hung down from it like a ribbon. Should this be correct, our earlier suggestion that the bar-su of the ED text stands for bar-si would thus be confirmed.

4. If the volute-like symbol of Inanna depicts a type of scarf, shawl, or band, one would then expect the sign MÙŠ to have a similar meaning. No such sense is documented for MÙŠ proper, whose only known meanings are „appearance" (Akk. *zīmu*) and „ground, territory, open land" (*mātu*),[39] both to be read mùš. However, the *gunû* variant of MÙŠ[40] (= MÚŠ) does actually denote a type of neck or head ornament, whose name was suh.[41] The verb regularly used in connection with suh is kešda (correctly: /kešedr/), „to tie, to fasten, to bind." In fact, this usage is so customary that there even exists a frozen compound suh-kešda, literally: „fastened suh" (Akk. *tiqnu*), which functions as a generic term for „ornament" or „adornment".[42] Among the attestations of suh, the following ones merit special interest:

(a) lugal sag-men-na hi-li-bi Šul-gi aga zi-da hé-du$_7$-bi suh-kešda nam-dingir-ra DU.DU, „king, the joy of the crown, Shulgi, the allure of the legitimate tiara, who *bears* the fastened suh of godship" (*Šulgi D* 8-10).

---

37 1 men-bar-su ... ^{d}Nanše (ibid. i 7 - ii 2).

38 For a similar conclusion, see J. Asher-Greve, AfO 42/43 (1995/96) 184 n. 22: „bar-su might refer to the covering of the substructure with a special material or to the appearance of the crown." Cf. also G. J. Selz, FAOS 15/2, p. 635, who too tends to connect bar-su with bar-si. See now Selz in I. L. Finkel and M. J. Geller (eds.), *Sumerian Gods and their Representations* (Groningen 1997), p. 190 n. 68: „I propose to take bar-su as a variant spelling of bar-si(g), translated by PSD B 126 as 'sash,' 'shawl.' men$_x$-bar-su may therefore tentatively be rendered as 'turban.'"

39 See Sjöberg, TCS 3, pp. 55-56.

40 Since MÙŠ-*gunû* is almost certainly a post-Uruk development (here note that ZATU-375, which M. W. Green, ATU 2, p. 249, interprets as MÙŠ-*gunû* is but an allograph of ZATU-374 = MÙŠ), it can be assumed that, in the Uruk script, the value /suh/ was attached to MÙŠ. The earliest attestations of MÙŠ-*gunû* come from ED sources. See, especially, its occurrence in the AbS/Ebla Geographical List line 115: Suh^{ki} (OIP 99 91 iv' 1) = Zú-hum^{ki} (MEE 3, p. 234).

41 For the conclusion that suh is a type of ornament, see Falkenstein, SGL 1, pp. 96-97; J. Renger, ZA 58 (1967) 127 („ein weiteres Zeichen der en-Würde war ein Schmuckstück, múš/mùš genannt, das umgebunden wurde"); Sjöberg, TCS 3, pp. 73, 92; Klein, *Three Šulgi Hymns* (Ramat-Gan 1981), pp. 90-91; Y. Sefati, *Studies Artzi*, p. 63 („SUH-kéš [*tiqnu*] is a sacred ornament, donned by kings and gods. Šulgi, e.g., wears this ornament, probably as a symbol of priesthood, along with the insignia of kingship. There are a number of deities in Sumerian mythology who also wear this ornament ...").

42 See na$_4$-suh-kešda = *ti-iq-nu* (MSL 10, p. 32 line 100); $^{su-ki-iš}$suh-keš(da) mah-a $^{ti-iq}$BAD-*iq-ni ṣi-ru-ti* (TCL 6 51 rev. 33f. = CAD Ṣ, p. 211b, S p. 342-43); suh^{su-uh}-kešda(!)(SAR) = *ti-iq-nu* (Antagal A 208 = MSL 17, p. 188); AHw., pp. 1360-1361; ù ki-sikil tur-re $^{su-ku}$(SUH.KEŠDA) ba-ni-in-AK^{na} (CT 58 42:79); and examples (a), (c), (e), (g) and (n) cited below.

(b) sig_4 $Eridug^{ki}$-ga-ta aga zi ak-me-en $Unug^{ki}$-ta $^{su\text{-}uh(!)}$suh za-gìn-na kéš-rá/-da-me-en, „in the brickwork of Eridu, I (Shulgi) am the legitimate tiara; in Uruk, I am the fastened lapis suh" (*Šulgi E* 10 = Klein, *Three Šulgi Hymns*, p. 90; Sefati, *Studies Artzi*, p. 63 n. 83).

(c) PN En-suh-kešda-an-na, „The en is the fastened suh of An/heaven" (D. O. Edzard, ZA 53 [1959] 18 n. 43; A. Berlin, OPBF 2, p. 65).

(d) lugal ù-tu suh zi kéš-dè/di en ù-tu sag-men gá-gá šu-na hé-en-gál / ì-gál, „to bring about the birth of a king, to tie (onto him) the legitimate suh, to bring about the birth of an en-priest(ess), to set a crown (upon his/her head), it is in her (Nintu's) power" (*Enki and the World Order* 197-198, 409-410; *Temple Hymns* 502-503).

(e) nu-gig An-na suh-kéšda gal-gal-la aga zi-dè ki-ág nam-en-na túm-ma, „(Inanna, you are) the nu-gig of An, (one) of great fastened suhs, lover of the legitimate tiara, suitable for enship" (*Ninmešarra* 3-4).

(f) nu-u_8-gig-ra suh(!)(MÙŠ) kéš-di, „she (Ninisina) ties a suh upon the nu-gig-priestess" (*Temple Hymns* 389).

(g) siki PA nam-en-na suh-kéš-da-gá, „the ... of enship, of my (i.e., of Suen's) fastened suh" (*Lamentation over Sumer and Ur* 458).

(h) ^{d}Nin-urta dumu ^{d}En-líl-lá-[k]e_4 nam-lugal-šè men mu-un-gùr ... nam-en-šè(!) suh za-gìn mu-un-kešda, „Ninurta, son of Enlil, put on a crown as a sign of kingship, tied on a lapis suh as a sign of enship" (SGL 1, p. 82 ii 15-16).

(i) en-e nam-en-šè suh mu-un-[kešda] nam-lugal-šè aga zi m[u-un-gùr], „the Lord (Enki) [tied on] the suh as a sign of enship, [put on] the legitimate tiara as a sign of kingship" (*Enki and the World Order* 263-264).

(j) eden-en-na men kug nam-mi-in-gùr an-eden-na su_6 za-gìn àm-lá suh za-gìn àm-kešda, „he (Enki) raised a holy crown over the *high* plain, he fastened a lapis beard to the high plain, tied upon it a lapis suh" (*Enki and the World Order* 348-349).

(k) gíg-ù-na suh(!)(MÙŠ) kéš-dè/di, „in the night he (Utu) ties on a suh" (*Temple Hymns* 490).

(l) ^{d}Utu an-na-ke_4 suh(!)(MÙŠ) za-gìn mu-un-kešda, „Utu of heaven tied on a lapis such" (*Gilgameš and Ḫuwawa B* 29).

(m) dìm giš-nu$_{11}$-gal suh za-gìn kešda hi-li-zu zé-ba-àm, „(Inanna to Dumuzi:) 'alabster figurine, fastened with a lapis suh, sweet is your allure!'" (SRT 31:32 = *Studies Artzi*, pp. 52-53).

(n) en suh-kešda hé-du$_7$ an-eden-na, „the Lord (Enkimdu) who has a suh fastened, the ornament of the high plain" (*Enki and the World Order* 321).

(o) kur-ku-rá-a-ni kur hé-gál sug$_4$ ki DU.DU-ni gissu-bi suh za:gìn-na-gim ab-šag$_4$-ga lá-a, „his (Enki's) flood-waves fill the land(s) with abundance; the shade of his 'place of standing' stretches into the midst of the sea like a lapis suh" (MDP 14, p. 125 lines 6-9 – a Sargonic incantation).

(p) suh nam-en-šè kug-ge-eš-e túm-ma, „(Enanedu, the en priestess of Nanna) fit for the suh of holy enship" (Iraq 13 [1951] 27 and pl. XIV line 7).

(q) lugal šuh-luh-luh-ha-ke$_4$ en suh en gal-la ^{d}En-ki-ke$_4$, „Enki, master of cleansing rites, the lord of the suh of the great en priest" (*Nisaba and Enki* 39).

As this evidence shows, the suh was an attribute of deities (both female and male), of kings, of en officials, and of nu-gig priestesses. As such, it apparently enjoyed a wide cultic application. At the same time, however, it is characteristic that it is mentioned most frequently in the contexts involving Inanna and her cult. Thus Inanna is identified as the one of great suh ornaments (e); Shulgi wears a suh when in Uruk (b); the name of Ensuhkeshdana, a mythical ruler of Uruk, invokes a suh (c); a suh is donned by a nu-gig priestess (f); the same is said of Dumuzi (m). This could argue for a special association of this ornament with Inanna's cult.

As for its specific meaning, we undoubtedly find here a type of band. Since suh is compared to „crown" (men) and „tiara" (aga), and since it may have been decorated with lapis-lazuli, it certainly was an object of considerable importance and value, which was worn over the head. A translation „diadem" would thus not be inappropriate.

5. To summarize our conclusions, in the ED passage in question the emblem (urin) of Inanna (= Inanna's volute-like symbol) is described as a lapis lazuli scarf (bar-si). That scarf was not unlike the „diadem" (suh), which is one of the meanings of MÙŠ/MÚŠ (a drawing of Inanna's volute-like symbol). It would seem, therefore, that the archaic symbol of Inanna depicts a scarf or head-band.[43]

---

[43] See now P.-A. Beaulieu's contribution in this volume pp. 25-26.

Such a possibility would certainly not be contradicted by the image itself, which, as matter of fact, can most plausibly be explained as a partially rolled-up long piece of fabric, with a loop and two loose ends, which is attached to the top of a pole (fig. 7).

A striking visual parallel for such a rolled-up piece of fabric is provided by the so-called „sacred knot" of Minoan Crete,[44] which is depicted in frescoes and on pottery, and whose models in faience and ivory were found at Knossos, Zakro and Mycenae (figs. 8 and 9).[45] This object „consisted of a strip of patterned cloth with a fringe at each end, a knotted loop in the middle and the two ends hanging down like a modern neck-tie."[46] Although the similarity[47] between the two symbols cannot but be accidental, it nevertheless is very instructive, for it suggests a common solution to the difficult problem of depicting a piece of fabric as an isolated, self-sustained object.

And, closer to our Honoree's home, one finds a 14th century A.D. coat-of-arms called Nałęcz, which too shows a knotted-up scarf, with its two loose ends hanging down (fig. 10).[48] By offering this last example I wish not only to underscore the universal nature of symbolic imagery, but also to provide Inanna's attire with some real „polish". (I hope that neither the Honoree nor her beloved Inanna will take offense for this silly pun!)

---

[44] I am indebted to D. R. Frayne for bringing this point to my attention, and for providing me with some of the literature (see the following two notes).

[45] See M. P. Nilsson, *The Minoan-Mycenaean Religion and its Survival in Greek Religion* (Lund 1949), pp. 162-163; S. Alexiou, *Contribution to the Study of the Minoan 'Sacred Knot'*, in W. C. Brice (ed.), *Europa: Studien zur Geschichte und Epigraphik der frühen Aegaeis, Festschrift für Ernst Grumach*, (Berlin 1967), pp. 1-6; E. Gullberg and P. Åströms, *The Thread of Ariadne: A Study of Ancient Greek Dress* (Göteborg 1970), pp. 21-22; M. Cameron, *The 'Palatial' Thematic System in the Knossos Murals: Last Notes on the Knossos Frescoes*, in R. Hägg and N. Marinatos (eds.), *The Function of the Minoan Palaces: Proceedings of the Fourth International Symposium at the Swedish Institute in Athens, 1984*, (Stockholm 1987), p. 324.

[46] R. Castleden, *Minoans: Life in Bronze Age Crete* (London 1990), p. 136.

[47] This similarity was noted already by Alexiou, op. cit., pp. 2, 4-6.

[48] This coat-of-arms belongs to over one hundred different families (among them, the family of the author's mother, the Nałęcz-Tański). See H. Stupnicki, *Herbarz polski i imionospis ... na podstawie Niesieckiego i manuskryptów*, vol. 1 (Lwów 1855), pp. 171-172.

LIST OF FIGURES

1. Cylinder seal. Warka. Uruk Period. After E. Heinrich, *Kleinfunde aus den archaischen Tempelschichten in Uruk* (Berlin 1936), pl. 18 fig. b.

2. Cylinder seal. Warka. Uruk period. After D. Collon, *First Impressions: Cylinder Seals in the Ancient Near East* (Chicago 1988), p. 174 no. 807.

3. Stone trough. Warka? Uruk period. After P. P. Delougaz, JNES 27 (1968) 187 fig. 5.

4. Clay frieze element. Warka. Uruk period. After Jordan, UVB 2 (Berlin 1931), p. 34 fig. 23.

5. Clay frieze element. Warka. Uruk period. After J. Jordan, UVB 1 (Berlin 1930), pl. 19 bottom.

6. Clay frieze element; collection of the Iraq Museum, Baghdad. Warka? Uruk period. After S. Alexiou, op. cit., pl. 1 no. 1.

7. Modern reconstruction of the volute-like symbol.

8. Ivory object from the South-East House at Knossos. After Alexiou, op. cit., pl. 1 no. 4.

9. Knot on the fresco from Nirou. After Alexiou, op. cit., pl. 1 no. 5.

10. Coat-of-arms Nałęcz. After Stupnicki, op. cit., p. 171.

Fig. 1

Fig. 2

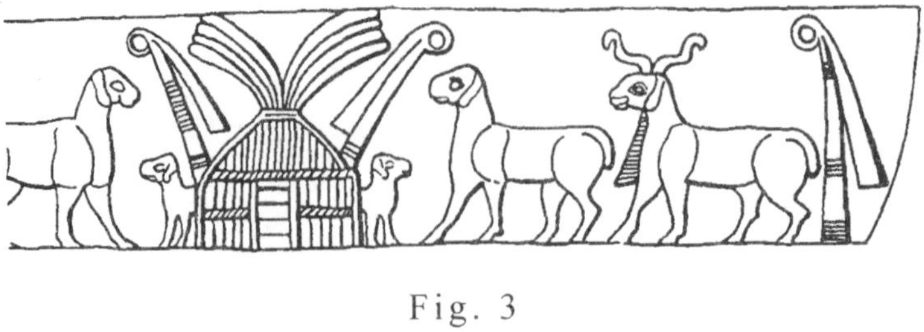

Fig. 3

Fig. 4

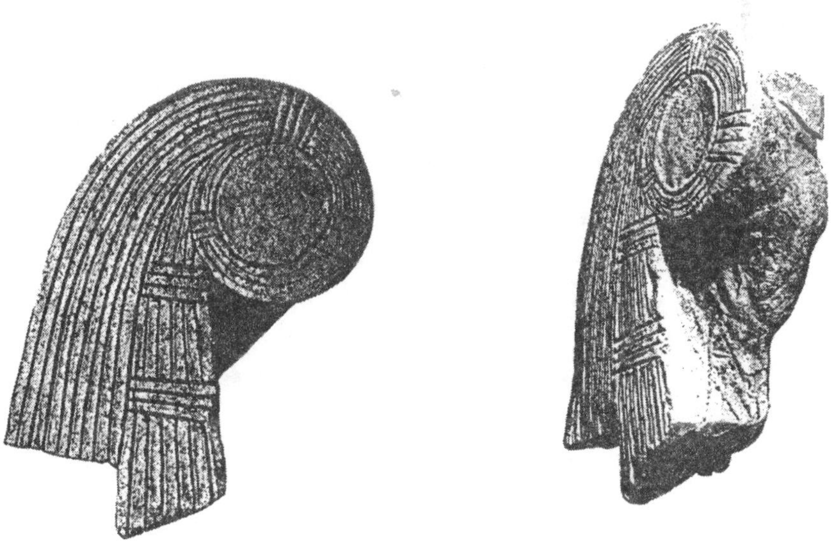

Fig. 5

Fig. 6

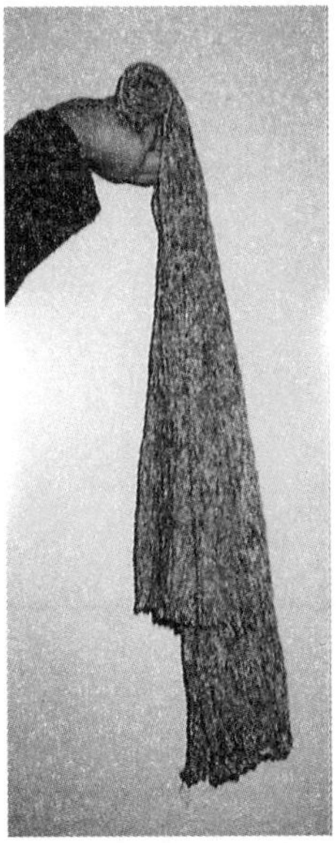

Fig. 7

Fig. 8

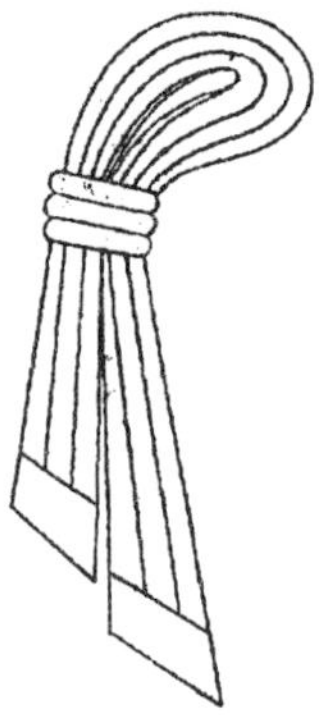

Fig. 9

Fig. 10

THREE NEO-SUMERIAN TEXTS FROM A PRIVATE COLLECTION IN POLAND

Marek Stępień

The tablets published in the present text come from a collection of Professor Romana Barnycz-Gupieniec of Łódź (formerly the collection of Mr. Anatol Gupieniec) and have not been studied so far.[1] The tablets are most probably of the same antique trade provenience as the collection of neo-Sumerian tablets belonging to the District Museum in Toruń.[2] This is confirmed by the information obtained from the collection owner as well as similarities between some elements of the contents of the two documents belonging to such small groups of texts, which may well testify to a single primary archive.[3]

The tablets originate from two Sumerian towns: Puzriš-Dagān (*Drehem*) and Umma (*Djokha*). The essence of the first two texts: B-G 1 and B-G , deserves attention. The first does so because of the supplier, the governor of Umma ($ensi_2$ $Umma^{ki}$) and the rather infrequent expression *gu-gu-tum* which refers to the handled animal. The second – because of the unusual article and its destination. The third document is a typical messenger text.

* * *

Tablet 1 (B-G 1)

Dimensions: 35 (width) x 41 (height) x 17 mm (thick)
Provenience: Puzriš-Dagān (*Drehem*)
Date: Š 45 / AS 2 . I
Contents: the supply of one fattened sheep by the governor of Umma

---

[1] It is my desire hereby to express my thanks to the owner of the collection, Professor Romana Barnycz-Gupieniec, for her permission to publish the collection.

[2] See M. Stępień, *Kolekcja neosumeryjskich tekstów klinowych w zbiorach Muzeum Okręgowego w Toruniu*, Rocznik Muzeum w Toruniu IX (1992) s. 63.

[3] In both texts from Drehem (Rocznik Muzeum w Toruniu IX 4 and the B-G 2 which is published here) the governor ($ensi_2$) of Umma is the goods supplier.

Remarks: very good condition, visible traces of changing the month date by the scribe.

1. Autography

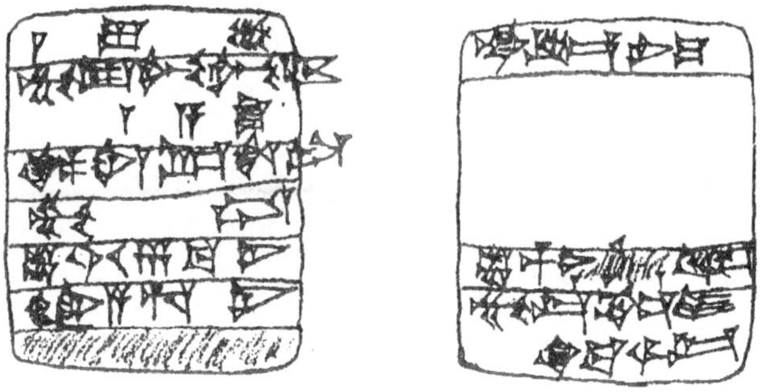

2. Transliteration	3. Translation
Obverse	
1. 1 udu niga	1 fattened sheep
2. mu sila$_4$ *gu-gu-tum* / 1-a-še$_3$	instead of a *gugutum*-lamb
3. ki ensi$_2$ Umma^{ki}-ta	from the governor of Umma
4. mu-DU	was delivered.
5. iti u$_4$-16 ba-zal	On the 16th day of the month.
6. gir$_3$ A-ḫu-ni	Via Ahuni
Reverse	
7. Na-ša$_6$ i$_3$-dab$_5$	Naša took it in charge.
(BLANK SPACE)	
8. iti maš-da$_3$-<erasure>-ku$_2$	The month of „eating gazelle”.
9. mu *Ur-bi$_2$-lum* /^{ki} ba-ḫul	Year: the town of Urbilum was destroyed.

4. Commentary

Line 2: The meaning of the expression *gu-gu-tum* is not quite clear, see AHw p. 296: *gugutum/dum* – „ein Futterkraut”; CAD G p. 123: *gugutum* – „a bread of sheep”. This term is very rarely found in the documents of Ur III period. Compare texts:

ASJ 15, 137,1-4: 1 udu niga, mu sila$_4$ *gu-gu-tum* 1-a-še$_3$, ki Nam-zi-tar-ra ensi$_2$ Gu-du$_8$-a^{ki}, mu-DU

AUCT 2, 375,10-12: [...] sila$_4$ *gu-gu-tum*-še$_3$, [...]-u,-mu-ta, [x Gu$_3$-d]e$_2$-a ensi$_2$ Gu$_2$-du$_8$-a^{ki}
JCS 14, 109,9-11: 1 udu, mu sila$_4$ *gu-gu-tum*-še$_3$, bala Šu-ma-ma ensi$_2$ Ka-zal-lu^{ki}
MVN 2, 159,5-10: 1 udu niga mu, ..., u$_3$ sila$_4$ *gu-gu-tum-ma*-še$_3$, ki Bēlum^{um}-i$_3$-li$_2$ sanga Utu Zimbir^{ki}-ta, mu-DU
PDT 1, 575,9: 6 sila$_4$ *gu-gu-tum*
RA 8, 185,3,1-5: 1 sila$_4$ ga *gu-gu-tum*, e$_2$ uz-ga, Da-a-nim maškim, (-), mu Ur-Lama ensi$_2$ Gir$_2$-su^{ki}-ka

As can be seen, this term is the description of young lamb which had often been exchanged into adult sheep (sometimes fattened with barley). It is noteworthy to remember that these animals had been often handled by provincial governors apparently as part of some obligatory payments to temples or administrative units which were getting supplies or settlements done by offices in Puzriš-Dagān. All the texts in which *gugutum*-lamb is present come from the archive of Puzriš-Dagān. It is, therefore possible that the text is about lambs (animal) fed or fattened in some special way, for some cult-related purposes.

Tablet 2 (B-G 2)

Dimensions: 42 (width) x 45 (height) x 17 mm (thick)
Provenience: Umma (*Djokha*)
Date: AS.4
Contents: confirmation of receipt of 4 stars decorations for the bronze doors of the god Šara's temple in Apišal
Remarks: the entire surface of the tablet is covered with the seal impressions of Šakuge, the son of Hešage, an exorcist-priest.

1. Autography

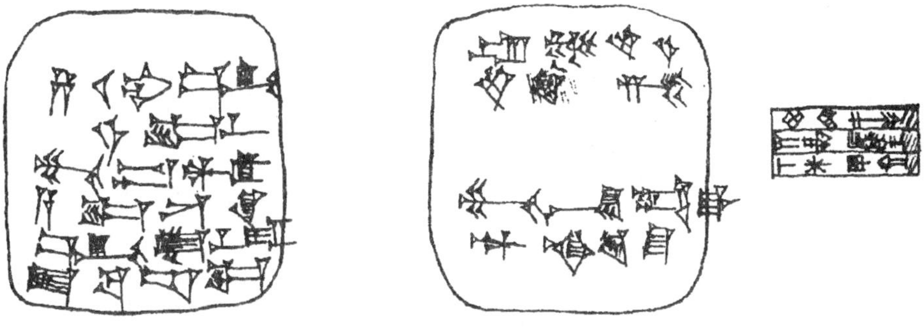

2. Transliteration	3. Translation
Obverse:	
1. 4 ul ^{giš}ig / zabar	4 stars (for) the door of bronze,
2. mu-DU ^{d}Šara$_2$	delivery (for) the god Šara
3. A-pi$_4$-šal^{ki}	of Apišal.
4. ^{giš}ig ka$_2$ bar-ra/-ke$_4$	The doors (for) the main gate
5. ba-ab-du$_{11}$	were destined (*literally*: ordered).
Reverse:	
6. kišib nam-ša$_3$-tam	(Receipt confirmed with) seal
7. Ša$_3$-ku$_3$-ge	of Šakuge.
(BLANK SPACE)	
8. mu En-maḫ-gal/-an-na ba-ḫun	Year: the Enmahgalanna was intronized.
Seal:	
Ša$_3$-ku$_3$-ge	Šakuge
dumu Ḫe$_2$-ša$_6$-g[e]	son of Hešage
išib ^{d}Ša[ra$_2$-k]a(?)	an exorcist-priest of the god Šara

4. Commentary

Line 1: The stars, probably also made of metal (bronze or copper) appear extremely rarely as an ornament in the neo-Sumerian source material. Compare H. Limet,[4] page 232, who quotes one document of Ur (UET III 327) which mentions 13 stars of copper which were most probably intended as throne decorations. Making the doors from bronze, e.g. for the temple of Haia at Ur, is confirmed by the UET III 688,2.[5]

Line 4: bar, here meaning *kawû* – „external", see: AHw p. 466 – examples of the usage of bar as a description of „external, main gate" – ka$_2$ bar-ra.

Tablet 3 (B-G 3)

Dimensions:	24 (width) x 28 (height) x 10 mm (thick)
Provenience:	Umma (*Djokha*)
Date:	AS.7.IV
Contents:	messenger-text
Remarks:	the tablet carries text on almost all it surface. Its upper and lower edges were particularly intensively used an, as a result, we now have almost a continuous text.

[4] H. Limet, *Le travail du métal au pays de Sumer au temps de la IIIe dynastie d'Ur* (Paris 1960).
[5] Op. cit., p. 214.

1. Autography

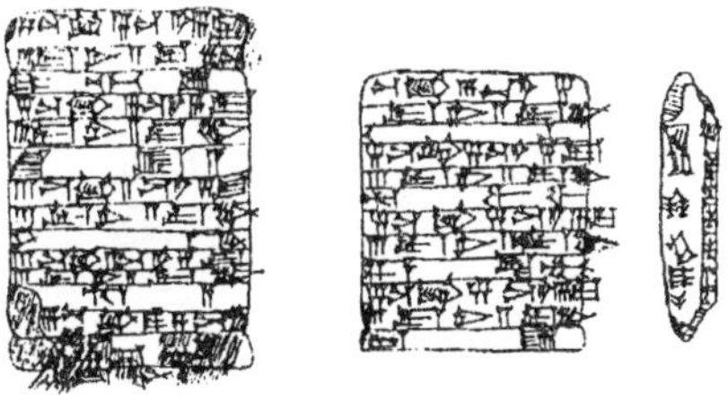

2. Transliteration	3. Translation
Obverse	
1. ⟨5⟩ sila$_3$ kaš 5 sila$_3$ [nin]da 5 ⟨gin$_2$ sum⟩	⟨5⟩ liters of beer, 5 liters of bread, 5 ⟨shekels of onion⟩
2. ⟨3⟩ gin$_2$ i$_3$ 2 gin$_2$ naga	⟨3⟩ shekels of oil, 2 shekels of alkali
3. U-bar	(for) Ubar
4. 5 sila$_3$ kaš 5 sila$_3$ ninda 5 gi[n$_2$] ⟨sum⟩	5 liters of beer, 5 liters of bread, 5 shekels ⟨of onion⟩,
5. 3 gin$_2$ i$_3$ 2 gin$_2$ [na]ga	3 shekels of oil, 2 shekels of alkali
6. Ḫu-wa-wa	(for) Huwawa
7. 5 sila$_3$ kaš 5 sila$_3$ ninda 5 gin$_2$ ⟨sum⟩	5 liters of beer, 5 liters of bread, 5 shekels ⟨of onion⟩,
8. 3 gin$_2$ i$_3$ 2 [gi]n$_2$ [na]ga	3 shekels of oil, 2 shekels of alkali
9. Kal-la-mu	(for) Kallamu
10. 5 sila$_3$ kaš 5 sila$_3$ ninda 5 gin$_2$ ⟨sum⟩	5 liters of beer, 5 liters of bread, 5 shekels ⟨of onion⟩,
11. 3 gin$_2$ i$_3$ 2 gin$_2$ naga	3 shekels of oil, 2 shekels of alkali
Lower edge	
12. [U]r?-sukkal	(for) Ur?-sukkal
Reverse	
13. [1+]4 sila$_3$ kaš 5 sila$_3$ ninda 5 g[in$_2$] ⟨sum⟩	5 liters of beer, 5 liters of bread, 5 shekels ⟨of onion⟩,
14. 3 gin$_2$ i$_3$ 2 gin$_2$ n[ag]a	3 shekels of oil, 2 shekels of alkali
15. I-ti-zu	(for) Itizu
16. 5 sila$_3$ kaš 5 sila$_3$ ninda 5 gin$_2$ ⟨sum⟩	5 liters of beer, 5 liters of bread, 5 shekels ⟨of onion⟩,
17. 3 gin$_2$ i$_3$ 2 gin$_2$ naga	3 shekels of oil, 2 shekels of alkali

18. Šu-E$_2$-a	(for) Šu-E$_2$a
19. 3 sila$_3$ kaš 2 sila$_3$ ninda 5 gin$_2$ ⟨sum⟩	3 liters of beer, 2 liters of bread, 5 shekels ⟨of onion⟩,
20. 3 gin$_2$ i$_3$ 2 gin$_2$ naga	3 shekels of oil, 2 shekels of alkali
21. Du$_{10}$-ga	(for) Duga
22. 3 sila$_3$ kaš 2 sila$_3$ ninda 5 gin$_2$ ⟨sum⟩	3 liters of beer, 2 liters of bread, 5 shekels ⟨of onion⟩,
23. 3 gin$_2$ i$_3$ 2 gin$_2$ naga	3 shekels of oil, 5 shekels of alkali
24. [*A*]-*ḫu-a*	(for) Ahua
25. [šu?-nigin$_2$? 0.0.3]6 sila$_3$ kaš 0.0.3 4 sila$_3$ ninda	[Total: 3]6 liters of beer, 34 liters of bread,
Upper edge	
26. [2/]3 sila$_3$ s[um]	2/3 liter of oni[on],
27. [1/]3 sila$_3$ 4 [gi]n$_2$ i$_3$	1/3 liter, 4 shekels of oil,
28. [1]6 [gi]n$_2$ naga	16 shekels of alkali.
Side edge	
29. [u]$_4$ 27-kam iti nesag$_2$	27th [day] of month nesag$_2$
30. mu Ḫu-ḫu-nu-ri^{ki}	Year: Huhunuri <was destroyed>.

4. Commentary

Line 1: the absence of the goods to which the amount of 5 shekels refers is found in every first line of the subsequent fragments of the text. Considering that the document comes from Umma, we should reckon that it refers to onion. A great many of Umma texts say the onion was among items issued to messengers and, according to a local writing manner (may be it was the same scribe) the sign SUM is often omitted as an understood – compare e.g.: AAS 29,10,13,16; AAS 30,4,10; AAS 31,5',18'; AAS 32,4,7; GDD 207, 7,10,13; GDD 299,7; KDD 42,1 passim; 43,1 and passim; 44,1 and passim; MVN XIV 197,1 and passim; Nik. II[6] 353,1 and passim; Umma III 1864,4 and passim; Watson II[7] 67,1 and passim.

Lines 1, 13: collation based on sum of line 25.

Line 12: the possible completion of the name, written as two signs of which the second is SUKKAL, is as follows: Dingir-sukkal, Lu$_2$-sukkal, Lugal-sukkal, Ur-sukkal. In connection with the visible traces of the first sign, the most probable name is Ur-sukkal. On the other hand, Lu$_2$-sukkal ra-gaba A-dam-dun^{ki} is know – see: texts Messenger[8] 332

Line 25: collation based on sum of lines 1, 4, 7, 10, 13, 16, 19, 22

---

[6] M.V. Nikol'skij, *Dokumenty chozjajstvennoj otčetnosti drevnej Chaldei iż sobranija N.P. Lichačeva, Čast'* II: *Epocha dinastii Agade i epocha dinastii Ura*, Drevnosti Vostočnyja 5, Moskva 1915

[7] P.J. Watson, *Neo-Sumerian Texts from Umma and other Sites* (Warminster 1993).

[8] M. Sigrist, *Messenger Texts from the British Museum* (Potomac 1990).

Line 27: collation based on sum of lines 2, 5, 8, 11, 14, 17, 20, 23
Line 28: collation based on sum of lines 2, 5, 8, 11, 14, 17, 20, 23
Line 29: one vertical visible before numeral 27.

A DOCUMENT FROM THE SECOND YEAR OF SIN-ŠAR-IŠKUN

by
Stefan Zawadzki
Poznań

The catalogue of Neo-Babylonian texts published by J. A. Brinkman and D. A. Kennedy, JCS 35 (1983) mentions the still unpublished document BM 49982 (83-3-23, 973) dated to the second year of Sin-šar-iškun, the last Neo-Assyrian king recognized in Babylonia. At present, the tablet measures 7,6 x 4,95 cm but the left side of the obverse is broken: only one or two signs are missing in lines 1-10 and 12, and a few more in line 13. At the begining of line 11, three erased (?) signs are still visible. The lower edge is broken and it is impossible to decide whether more lines are broken off. On the reverse, the left side of lines 1-3 and one or two signs from lines 4-11 are missing. The signs are clear and not difficult to read, except for a few ones which are poorly preserved. The tablet deserves to be published because its date can be used in reconstructing the chronology of the last period of the Assyrian presence in Babylonia. It is published here with the kind permission of the Trustees of the British Museum.

1. ZÚ.LUM.MA SUM^{nu} lúMU.MEŠ
2. [*in*]*a ma-ak-ka-su šá* ITU.BÁR EN ITU.ŠU

---

3. [x +] 7 DÚG*ma-ši-ḫu* m*Ib-na-a*
4. [x] EN 8 KIMIN *šá* mTIN-*su iš-šu-ú*
5. [x] KI.MIN mdEN-IM.TUKU
6. [x]⌈KI.MIN⌉ m*Zi-ka-ri*
7. [ŠE].BAR *ina* GIŠ.BÁN m*Ku-na-a*

---

8. [*as*?]-*ni-e* m*Ib-na-a* A-*šú šá* mNÍG.DU
9.] UD.15.KÁM meš (sic!) *a-pil*
10.]-*e ina* IGI mdEN-IM.TUKU
11. [erasure of four or five signs] *ina* IGI m*Ku-na-a*

12.] *qa* ZÚ.LUM.MA m*Ib-na-a*

13. GU]D$^{?}$ UD.8.KÁM

Rev.

1'] x x

2'] x x x *gu-qu-ú*

3' IT]U.BÁR *a-pil*

4' [x *ma*]-*ši-ḫu šá* ZÍZ.A.AN ^{m}*Zi-kar*

5' [x KI.MI]N ^{md}EN-IM.TUKU

6' [x KI.MI]N ^{m} x[

7' [x] KI.MIN 1 BÁN *ina* GIŠ.BÁN ^{m}TIN-*su*

8' [x KÙ]R 2 PI ŠE.GIŠ.Ì ^{m}BA^{šá}-a

9' [*gi*]-*nu-ú šá* ITU.BÁR *u* ITI.GUD *a-pil*

(A space for one line)

10. IT]U.GUD UD.8.KÁM ⸢MU⸣.2.KÁM

11. $^{m⸢d⸣}$30-LUGAL-GAR^{un}

(One line erased)

1. [Document$^{?}$] concerning the dates which were given (to) the bakers
2. from the choice quality dates from the month of Nisanu till the month of Du'uzu.

---

3. ⸢9?⸣ measures (for) Ibnâ
4. [x] together with eight measures which were delivered by Balassu.
5. [x] measures (for) Bēl-na'id
6. [x] measures (for) Zikari
7. - the barley in the *sūtu*-measure of Kunâ

---

8. ... of Ibnâ, son of Kudurru
9. [...] on fifteenth day is paid
10. ... at the disposal of Bēl-na'id
11. ... at the disposal of Kunâ.

---

12. [...] qa of dates (for) Ibnâ
13. [................] on the eighth day

Rev.

1' [.....]...

2' [......] *guqqu-* offering

3' [........of the mo]nth of Nisanu is paid.

4' [x mea]sures of emmer (for) Zikari
5' [x measur]es (for) Bēl-na'id
6' [x measur]es (for) ...
7' [x] measures, one *sūtu* in the *sūtu*-measure of Balassu

8' [x mea]sures, two *sūtu* of sesame (for) Iqīša
9' [as the *gi*]*nû*-offering for the month of Nisanu and Aiaru is paid.

---

10. Month of Aiaru, eighth day, second year
11. of Sin-šar-iškun.

Commentary:

1-2. The wording of these lines is strange because of the sequence of particular words and the lack of the verb. It is worth noting that the heading does not correspond fully with the contents of the whole text, where the deliveries of emmer and sesame are also counted.

8. At the beginning of the line one can expect the sign *gi* or *as.*

9. The sign *meš* is very clear. Maybe UD.15.KÁM is used here for *šapattu*, a period of fifteen days or a half of the month (cf. CAD Š I 449 f.).

11. One can see the signs *x ni e* at the beginning of the line. x cannot be identified with *gi* or *as.*

13. Before UD, a very small fragment of two oblique(?) signs is pre-served.

Rev.
1. Fragment of two signs.
2. Two or three signs before *quqqu.*
6. Fragmentarily preserved sign, maybe *kur* or *sila.*

The text is divided into six parts, with the heading and dating at the end of the text, but without the place of issue, which is typical for administrative texts.[1] The main part of the text includes a list of deliveries for particular persons, measured both in *mašiḫu* and *sūtu.* The deliveries comprise barley, dates, emmer and sesame. Comparison of lines 3-7 with Rev. 4-7 suggests that the same persons are named in both entries; the reason for division could be the fact that the first entry concerns barley, and the second one emmer. The exact sense of lines 8-13 and Rev. 1-3 is not clear, although Ibnâ, son of Kudurru, is certainly identical with Ibnâ of lines 3 and 12. It is interesting that

[1] Delete [...] in Brinkman-Kennedy's catalogue.

deliveries were measured according to the *sūtu*-measure of Kunâ or Balassu. The mentioning of *guqqu* in Rev. 2 ; and [*gi*]*nû* in Rev. 9', and maybe in Obv. 8, indicates that the products were used to prepare meals for the gods. The most important question is the following: who are the persons mentioned in the text? On the basis of the first line, the identification with the bakers seems sure, although the sequence of words in lines 1-2 looks strange. In the light of the recently published book by H. Bongenaar[2] who, however, does not mention this text, it is clear that the document was written in Sippar, and that the persons referred to are closely connected with the Ebabbar temple.[3] We can safely say that Sin-šar-iškun was recognized in Sippar on the 8th of Aiaru of his second year.

---

[2] A.C.V.M Bongenaar, *The Neo-Babylonian Ebabbar Temple at Sippar: its Administration and its Prosopography* (Leiden 1997).

[3] Op. cit. p. 175 (for Ibna) and add there „son of Kudurru" ... and make appropriate change in branch VII; p. 175 (Balassu; in light of our text his activity started a few year earlier); p. 199 (Zikar), p. 190 (Iqīša). Kuna is most probably identical with Kina (p. 190). Bēl-na'id is noted here for the first time, and because all other persons of our text belonged to the Isinnaya family, it is very likely the same for him.